MW01178757

Ra'Spee

Caring for the
Present Need
in the Lord's
Recovery

The
Holy
Word
for
Morning
Revival

Witness Lee

Living Stream Ministry
Anaheim, CA • www.lsm.org

First Edition, June 2007.

ISBN 0-7363-3476-9

Published by

Living Stream Ministry
2431 W. La Palma Ave., Anaheim, CA 92801 U.S.A.
P. O. Box 2121, Anaheim, CA 92814 U.S.A.

Printed in the United States of America

07 08 09 10 11 / 7 6 5 4 3 2 1

Contents

Week	Title	Page
	Preface	v

2007 Memorial Day Weekend Conference

**CARING FOR THE PRESENT NEED
IN THE LORD'S RECOVERY**

Week	Title	Page
	Title and General Subject	1
1	**Walking in the Truth of the Economy of God, Realizing the Recovery of the Lord, and Staying Away from Death and Division**	
	Outline	2
	Day 1	8
2	**Knowing the Present Truth, Upholding the Absoluteness of the Truth, and Being Constituted with the Truth for the Church as the Pillar and Base of the Truth**	
	Outline	22
	Day 1	26
3	**Caring for the Oneness of the Body of Christ by Seeing, Experiencing, and Applying Twelve Crucial Matters**	
	Outline	40
	Day 1	46
4	**The Lord's Recovery of Prophesying as the Excelling Gift for the Building Up of the Church as the Body of Christ**	
	Outline	60
	Day 1	64

Week	Title	Page
5	**Responding to Christ's Heavenly Intercession by Praying at the Golden Incense Altar**	
	Outline	78
	Day 1	82
6	**Having a Clear View concerning the Present Situation and the Present Need in the Lord's Recovery**	
	Outline	96
	Day 1	102
	Recovery Version Reading Schedules:	
	Old Testament	116
	New Testament	120
	Daily Verse Cards	125

Preface

1. This book is intended as an aid to believers in developing a daily time of morning revival with the Lord in His word. At the same time, it provides a limited review of the Memorial Day weekend conference held in St. Paul, Minnesota, May 25-28, 2007. Through intimate contact with the Lord in His word, the believers can be constituted with life and truth and thereby equipped to prophesy in the meetings of the church unto the building up of the Body of Christ.

2. The entire content of this book is taken primarily from the published conference outlines, the text and footnotes of the Recovery Version of the Bible, selections from the writings of Witness Lee and Watchman Nee, and *Hymns,* all of which are published by Living Stream Ministry.

3. The book is divided into weeks. One conference message is covered per week. Each week presents first the message outline, followed by six daily portions, a hymn, and then some space for writing. The message outline has been divided into days, corresponding to the six daily portions. Each daily portion covers certain points and begins with a section entitled "Morning Nourishment." This section contains selected verses and a short reading that can provide rich spiritual nourishment through intimate fellowship with the Lord. The "Morning Nourishment" is followed by a section entitled "Today's Reading," a longer portion of ministry related to the day's main points. Each day's portion concludes with a short list of references for further reading and some space for the saints to make notes concerning their spiritual inspiration, enlightenment, and enjoyment to serve as a reminder of what they have received of the Lord that day.

4. The space provided at the end of each week is for composing a short prophecy. This prophecy can be composed by considering all of our daily notes, the "harvest" of our inspirations during the week, and preparing a main point with some sub-points to be spoken in the church

meetings for the organic building up of the Body of Christ.

5. Following the last week in this volume, we have provided reading schedules for both the Old and New Testaments in the Recovery Version with footnotes. These schedules are arranged so that one can read through both the Old and New Testaments of the Recovery Version with footnotes in two years.

6. As a practical aid to the saints' feeding on the Word throughout the day, we have provided verse cards at the end of the volume, which correspond to each day's scripture reading. These may be removed and carried along as a source of spiritual enlightenment and nourishment in the saints' daily lives.

7. The conference message outlines were compiled by Living Stream Ministry from the writings of Witness Lee and Watchman Nee. The outlines, footnotes, and references in the Recovery Version of the Bible are by Witness Lee. All of the other references cited in this publication are from the published ministry of Witness Lee and Watchman Nee.

Memorial Day Weekend Conference

(May 25-28, 2007)

General Subject:

Caring for the Present Need in the Lord's Recovery

Banners:

We must walk in the truth of the economy of God,
realize the recovery of the Lord,
and stay away from death and division.

We need to know the present truth,
uphold the absoluteness of the truth, and
be constituted with the truth for the church
as the pillar and base of the truth.

The ground of oneness is the processed and
consummated Triune God applied to our being, and
the essence of the genuine oneness is life and light.

We must receive the Lord's mercy to be
His overcomers who bring in a new revival
to turn the age in the Lord's recovery by arriving
at the highest peak of the divine revelation,
by living the life of a God-man, and
by shepherding people according to God
in the vital groups for the building up
of the Body of Christ.

*Walking in the Truth of the Economy of God,
Realizing the Recovery of the Lord, and
Staying Away from Death and Division*

Scripture Reading: Acts 26:16-19; 1 Tim. 1:3-6; 6:3-4; 2 Cor.
11:2-3; Rom. 16:17; 2 Tim. 4:22

Day 1

I. **We must walk in the truth of the heavenly
vision of God's economy, the mark of God's
economy, and the goal of God's economy; this
vision must be renewed in us day by day to
be the controlling vision of all our living,
work, and activity (Prov. 29:18a; Acts 26:16-19;
1 John 1:7; 3 John 3-4):**

A. God's economy is His plan to dispense Himself
into His chosen, predestinated, and redeemed
people as their life, their life supply, and their
everything to produce, constitute, and build up
the organic Body of Christ (1 Tim. 1:3-6; 6:3-4;
2 Cor. 11:2-3; Titus 1:9; Col. 2:19).

B. The mark of God's economy, the strategic and
central point of God's economy, is the indwelling,
subjective Christ as the Spirit in our spirit, our
mingled spirit (2 Cor. 3:17; 2 Tim. 4:22; Rom. 8:16;
1 Cor. 6:17):

1. We must be narrowed down and even zeroed
in to the all-inclusive divine Spirit in our
human spirit so that we may be kept from
missing the mark of the divine economy
(1 Tim. 1:6; Mal. 2:15-16; Rom. 1:9; 8:4, 6; Gal.
5:25; Phil. 3:3; 2 Cor. 2:13).

2. In the "blueprint" of God's original intention, man is the center of the entire universe, and the center of man is his spirit
(Gen. 2:7; Prov. 20:27):

a. The heavens are for the earth, the earth
is for man, and man was created by God
with a spirit so that he may contact
God, receive God, contain God, worship

God, live God, fulfill God's purpose for God, express God, and be one with God (Zech. 12:1; John 4:24).

  b. Without God being the Spirit and without our having a spirit to contact God, to be one with God, the whole universe is empty and we are nothing (Eccl. 1:2; 3:11; Job 32:8; cf. Rom. 9:21, 23; 2 Cor. 4:7).

 3. Christ as the life-giving Spirit can be everything to us when we live in and exercise our spirit; to live in our soul is to live in the principle of antichrist (Zech. 4:6; 12:1; 1 Cor. 15:45b; 6:17; 1 John 2:18-19).

Day 2
&
Day 3

 4. The Lord's recovery is the recovery of the oneness in our spirit; to be in our spirit is to be in Jerusalem, the place of simplicity and oneness, whereas to be in our mind is to be in Babylon, the place of confusion and division (John 4:24; Eph. 2:22; Rom. 1:9; 2 Tim. 1:6-7).

 5. Our spirit is a "country" of grace to swallow up race for the one new man; our mind is a "country" of quarreling; to enjoy the Lord as the Spirit in our spirit is to have grace with us; when this is lost, the degradation of the church is present (4:22; Gal. 6:18; 5:15; Col. 3:10-11).

 C. The goal of God's eternal economy is the reality of the organic Body of Christ, consummating in the New Jerusalem (Eph. 1:22-23; Rev. 21:2-3, 9-10):

  1. Without the local churches, there is no practical expression of the Body of Christ and there can be no reality of the Body of Christ (1:10-13; 2:7).

  2. God's eternal economy is to obtain the Body of Christ; any work outside of this is not in the central lane of God's economy (Eph. 4:1-6, 11-16).

   3. We must follow the footsteps of the apostle
      Paul to bring all the saints into the blend-
      ing life of the entire Body of Christ (1 Cor.
      12:24; Rom. 16:1-20).
   4. For the Lord's recovery in this age, we must
      cooperate with the Lord to be the over-
      comers as today's Zion in today's Jerusa-
      lem (the church life) for the building up of
      the Body of Christ to consummate the
      New Jerusalem (Rev. 3:21-22; 14:1-5; Judg.
      5:15-16, 31).
D. Teachings that differ from the unique and
   healthy teaching of God's economy, the teaching
   of the apostles, separate us from the genuine
   appreciation, love, and enjoyment of the precious person of the Lord Jesus Christ Himself as
   our life and our everything (1 Tim. 1:3-4; Acts
   2:42; 2 Cor. 11:2-3).
E. Today we can be in one accord because we have
   only one vision, the vision of the eternal economy of God (Acts 1:14; 1 Cor. 1:9-10; Jer. 32:39).

Day 4   II. **God's economy was unveiled through the
       apostles, but because the believers lost
       the proper understanding of God's econ-
       omy, there is the need for it to be recovered
       by the Lord:**
   A. The words *recovery* and *economy* refer to one
      thing as seen from two different viewpoints—
      with God it is a matter of economy; with us it is a
      matter of recovery (1 Tim. 1:4; Eph. 1:10; 3:9).
   B. *Recovery* means to go back to the beginning; we
      need to go back to the beginning, receiving the
      Lord's grace to go back to God's original inten-
      tion, to what God ordained in the beginning
      (Matt. 19:8).
   C. There is a strong and solid principle that
      whenever the majority of the people of God
      fail to carry out God's purpose, God comes in to
      have a recovery; His recovery is always with

the minority, with a remnant of overcomers, not with the majority (2 Kings 22:8; Ezra 1:3-11; Neh. 2:11, 17; Rev. 3:21; 18:4).

D. Our vision should be governed not by the present situation nor by traditional practice but by God's original intention and standard as revealed in the Scriptures according to the present advance of His recovery:

1. The Lord's recovery is the recovery of Christ as our center, reality, life, and everything (Col. 1:17b, 18b; Rev. 2:4, 7, 17; 3:20; Psa. 80:1, 15, 17-19).

2. The Lord's recovery is the recovery of the oneness of the Body of Christ (John 17:11, 21-23; Eph. 4:3-4a; Rev. 1:11).

3. The Lord's recovery is the recovery of the function of all the members of the Body of Christ (Eph. 4:15-16; 1 Cor. 14:4b, 26, 31).

E. We in the Lord's recovery must have a clear vision of God's economy and then be governed, controlled, and directed by this vision, for we are here to carry out God's economy in His recovery (Acts 26:18-19; Prov. 29:18a).

Day 5 **III. In order to realize the recovery of the Lord for the carrying out of the economy of God, we must stay away from division and death:**

A. We must stay away from death and be swallowed up by Christ as life; everything in the church must be in the nature of life, with the content of life, and in the flow and imparting of life (Num. 6:1-9; Lev. 5:2; 2 Cor. 5:4; John 7:38; 1 John 5:16a).

B. We must reject any kind of division (1 Cor. 1:10), stand against any wind of teaching and any spreading of spiritual death (Eph. 4:14; 2 Tim. 2:16-17), and mark and turn away from those who make divisions and causes of stumbling contrary to the teaching of God's economy (Rom. 16:17; Titus 3:10).

C. Leviticus reveals that the first thing that we as God's priests need to deal with is our listening; our moving (feet) and working (hands) are always under the direction of our hearing (8:23-24; 14:14-17):

 1. If we do not take care of our hearing but give ear to negative speaking, our deeds and our work will be affected in a negative way.

 2. If any church would stop hearing negative things, that church would be very healthy and living; the church that is the weakest and the most deadened is the one that is full of criticism, gossip, and reasoning.

 3. Because we often hear unclean things, things that are unhealthy and contagious, we need to wash our ears with the blood of Christ; after the washing of the blood, we will enjoy the anointing of the Spirit.

 4. Positive listening will rescue us from negative listening; if we listen to God's word from morning to evening, we will not have an ear to listen to any negative speaking (Rev. 2:7; John 10:3-5, 16, 27; S. S. 2:8, 14).

Day 6 D. In order to enjoy Christ as our meal offering to live a meal-offering church life, we must be purified from any leaven (ambition for leadership) and honey (natural affection) (Lev. 2:11):

 1. Ambition and natural affection go together; a person who is ambitious will love anyone who helps him to gain what he desires, but whoever hinders him from fulfilling his ambition will be regarded as his enemy (3 John 9).

 2. We should neither take the way of the Lord's recovery nor leave this way because of any person; we are following the vision of God's economy in the realization of the Lord's recovery (Acts 26:19; 2 Tim. 1:15; 2:1-15).

E. For us to live a holy life for the church life, we must be careful about the kind of people we contact; in Leviticus 11 all the animals signify different kinds of people, and eating signifies our contacting of people (cf. Acts 10:9b-15, 27-29):

1. To eat is to contact things outside of us and to receive them into us with the result that they eventually become our inner constitution; whatever we contact we will receive, and whatever we receive will reconstitute us, making us a different person from what we are now.

2. "Do not be deceived: Evil companionships corrupt good morals" (1 Cor. 15:33).

3. "He who walks with wise men will be wise, / But the companion of fools will be troubled" (Prov. 13:20).

4. "Avoid profane, vain babblings, for they will advance to more ungodliness, and their word will spread like gangrene, of whom are Hymenaeus and Philetus, who concerning the truth have misaimed...But flee youthful lusts, and pursue righteousness, faith, love, peace with those who call on the Lord out of a pure heart" (2 Tim. 2:16-18, 22).

Morning Nourishment

1 Tim.   Even as I exhorted you...to remain in Ephesus in
1:3-4   order that you might charge certain ones not to teach
         different things nor to give heed to myths and unend-
         ing genealogies, which produce questionings rather
         than God's economy, which is in faith.

[First Timothy 1:4 speaks of God's economy. The word *economy*]
primarily signifies the household management, the household
administration, arrangement and distribution, or dispensation (of
wealth, property, affairs, etc.). It is used with the intention of stress-
ing the focal point of God's divine enterprise, which is to distribute,
or dispense, Himself into man.

The three persons in the Godhead are for God's economy, the
divine distribution, the holy dispensation. The Father as the source
is embodied in the Son, and the Son as the course is realized in the
Spirit as the transmission. God the Father is Spirit (John 4:24), and
God the Son, as the last Adam, became a life-giving Spirit (1 Cor.
15:45). All is in God the Spirit, which is the Holy Spirit revealed in
the New Testament. This Holy Spirit today, with the fullness of the
Father in the riches of the Son, has come into our human spirit and
dwells there to impart all that God is into our very being. This is
God's economy, the divine dispensing. The Holy Spirit of God,
dwelling in our human spirit to dispense all that God is in Christ
into our being, is the focus, the very mark of this mysterious distribution of the Triune God. This is the battleground of the spiritual
warfare. Oh, how much the subtle enemy has been and still is dis-
tracting the saints of God, even the seeking ones, from this mark of
God's economy by so many good and even scriptural things. In such
a time of confusion, as in the time when the Epistles to Timothy
were written, we must be narrowed down and even zeroed in to
the all-inclusive divine Spirit in our human spirit that we may be
kept from missing the mark of the divine economy. Therefore, the
returning to, the abiding in, and the exercising of our spirit to realize the Spirit of God is a basic necessity today. It is by so doing
that we may partake of all the fullness of God by enjoying the
unsearchable riches of Christ. (*The Economy of God,* pp. 5-6)

Today's Reading

God and Christ have come to dwell in our spirit....Second Timothy 4:22 [says]: "The Lord be with your spirit."...Ephesians 4:6 [says that] God the Father is in us; Second Corinthians 13:5, [that] God the Son is in us; and Romans 8:11, [that] God the Spirit is in us. The Triune God in the persons of the Father, the Son, and the Spirit is now in our spirit. Here is the mark of God's economy: the Triune God is in our spirit to be our life and everything. Oh, how God's economy has been neglected in the past centuries by His children! We must recover this mark of God in our spirit.

Using our spirit as His center, God works Himself out through us....Now the Triune God and all that He has accomplished are in our spirit as our life and everything. From this central point the Triune God spreads out to saturate the inward parts of our being with Himself. The human spirit is the very...mark of God's economy. ...I do not say this is the *goal* of God's economy, but the *mark*. This mark has been neglected by most Christians today....We must realize that all the teachings of the sixty-six books of the Bible are for this mark. All the different gifts and all the different functions are for this mark and must be centered upon this mark. (*The Economy of God,* p. 212)

If we did not have a spirit, we would be like the beasts....The key to our meaning...is...in our having a spirit. God is Spirit and we must contact Him, worship Him, in our spirit (John 4:24). These two spirits should contact each other and should become one (1 Cor. 6:17). Then the whole universe becomes meaningful. Then our life has its meaning. Without God being the Spirit and without us having a spirit to contact God, to be one with God, the whole universe is empty and we are nothing. By this we can see the importance of our spirit. (*The Spirit with Our Spirit,* p. 78)

Further Reading: The Economy of God, chs. 1, 4-5, 24; *The Practice of the Church Life according to the God-ordained Way,* ch. 1; *Life-study of Job,* msgs. 19, 24, 27; *The Vision of the Age,* chs. 2-3

Enlightenment and inspiration: _____

_____

_____

_____

Morning Nourishment

John   God is Spirit, and those who worship Him must wor-
4:24   ship in spirit and truthfulness.
2 Tim.   The Lord be with your spirit. Grace be with you.
  4:22

The Lord Jesus told [the] Samaritan woman that the proper
worship is neither on a certain mountain nor at Jerusalem, but
today the worship to God must be in our spirit (John 4:21, 24).

Our spirit is today's Jerusalem. We may have a lot of different
opinions and dissenting concepts in our mind, but when we turn
ourselves from our mind to our spirit, right away we are one....In
our mind we have the principle of Babylon. But in our spirit we
have the principle of Jerusalem....The exercise of the mind leads
to quarreling and debating and eventually to division with confusion. When you are in the mind, you are in Babylon. We must turn
ourselves from the mind to the spirit. When we get into our spirit,
we are one. Then there is no more division or confusion. Today's
Jerusalem is our spirit. It is here that we have God's habitation. It
is here that we call upon His precious name. The Lord's name and
His habitation today are in our spirit. (*The Living and Practical
Way to Enjoy Christ*, p. 56)

Today's Reading

In the beginning the saints were focused on the divine Spirit
mingled with their human spirit—the mingled spirit (Rom. 8:16;
1 Cor. 6:17; Rom. 8:4)....[They] were in the spirit enjoying Christ,
experiencing Christ, and expressing Christ in a corporate way.
That was the church life in the beginning. In this proper church
life, there were no religion, no outward regulations, no rituals, and
no vain doctrines or teachings. The saints were exercised to be in
the spirit to enjoy Christ, to experience Christ, and to express and
speak Christ in a corporate way.

The Lord's recovery is to bring us up out of a fallen situation...to His divine standard. The more we are brought up, the
simpler we become [and]...the more we become nothing.

In books such as Romans and Ephesians, there are many
teachings, but in Revelation there is just the spirit—the sevenfold

intensified Spirit of God (1:4; 4:5; 5:6) and the human spirit (1:10; 4:2; 17:3; 21:10). John was in spirit and he saw the golden lampstands—one lampstand for one city (1:10-12)....This is so simple. The many believers in a city should be just one lampstand in one accord, without disputation, different opinions, or different concepts and divisions. Thank the Lord that we are here today standing in oneness, but in our hearts we may still hold on to something of ourselves and something other than Christ. In God's eyes, a local church must be so simple. It should be a lampstand of pure gold without mixture—so simple, single, and pure....The Lord desires something fully in the spirit.

The book of Revelation is a book of the Spirit and the bride. The church is something absolutely in the Spirit. We need to turn to our spirit and stay in our spirit. In the spirit we are one. Nothing is as important or as strategic in the New Testament as the oneness of the believers. The Lord Jesus prayed that we all would be one (John 17:21). Some maintain that they want to be scriptural, but in their exercise to be scriptural, they divide the saints. Nothing is more unscriptural than to divide the saints. It is better to have a whole man who is dirty than a clean, dismembered arm of a man. The arm being clean may be likened to being "scriptural." Although the arm is clean, it is...divided from the body.

Our need today is to be in the Spirit and in the Body, in the Spirit and in the oneness. We should care only for being in the Spirit and in the Body. This is what the Lord has been doing among us and with us throughout our history. Year after year the Lord has been gaining something because we are becoming clearer that the Lord's desire is absolutely a matter of our being in the Spirit and in the Body. (*The History of the Church and the Local Churches,* pp. 131-132)

Further Reading: The Living and Practical Way to Enjoy Christ, ch. 8; The History of the Church and the Local Churches, chs. 9-10; How to Be a Co-worker and an Elder and How to Fulfill Their Obligations, ch. 3; Living in the Spirit, ch. 5

Enlightenment and inspiration: _____
_____
_____

Morning Nourishment

Eph. ...**The church, which is His Body, the fullness of the**
1:22-23 **One who fills all in all.**

We may think that the local churches are the goal of God's economy. However, they are not the goal but the procedure God takes to
reach the goal of His economy....Since the time of Brother Nee the
local churches have become a very precious item in our Christian
life. Some of the saints may be disappointed when they hear that the
local churches are not God's goal. Nevertheless, if we are just in
the local churches and do not go on, we are far off from God's goal.

According to Ephesians 1:22-23, the goal of God's economy is the
church, which is Christ's Body....We are in the church; that is a fact.
But where is the reality of the Body of Christ? We have the term *the
Body of Christ* and we have the doctrine of the Body of Christ, but
where is the practicality and reality of the Body of Christ?

We all need to consider this matter. We have the term and we
have the doctrine, but practically, we do not have the reality. The
purpose of the blending is to usher us all into the reality of the Body
of Christ. I treasure the local churches, as you do. But I treasure the
local churches because of a purpose. The local churches are the procedure to bring me into the Body of Christ. (*The Practical Points
concerning Blending*, pp. 9-10)

Today's Reading

The last three chapters of Romans show us that we need to
reign in life particularly in two crucial matters. The first thing is in
imitating the apostle to bring the local churches into the fellowship
of the Body of Christ (Rom. 14:3; 15:7-9, 25-33); the second thing is
in following in the apostle's footsteps to bring all the saints into the
blending life of the entire Body of Christ (ch. 16).

In imitating the apostle to bring the local churches into the fellowship of the Body of Christ, we must learn not to despise or judge others in their doctrines or practices according to doctrinal concepts,
religious practices, and anything that is unrelated to our basic faith.

We should receive people according to God's receiving, not being
more narrow than God, thereby demonstrating and maintaining

the oneness of the Body of Christ. Furthermore, we should receive people according to the Son of God, according to God, not according to doctrine or practice, thus maintaining a condition of absolute peace, smoothness, and order, without any deviation and discord, in the fellowship of the Body of Christ to the glory of God (Rom. 14:3; 15:7).

We have much to learn concerning receiving people according to God and according to His Son. Because of our negligence in this matter in the past, we have offended the Body of Christ and many brothers and sisters in the Lord. For this reason, I had a deep repentance before the Lord. Brothers and sisters, I hope that we can see our past mistakes by getting into this message through pray-reading, studying, reciting, and prophesying. Of course, sectarianism in the denominations is wrong; it is something very much condemned by God. Nevertheless, those who are genuinely saved in the denominations are children of God and have been received by God. Hence, we also should receive them, but we would never participate in the division in which they are.

We [also] must follow in the footsteps of the apostle. He brought us into the blending life of the entire Body of Christ by recommendations and greetings that the God of peace may crush Satan under our feet and that we may enjoy the rich grace of Christ (vv. 1-16, 21-24, 20). In Romans 16 the apostle Paul greeted the saints, one by one, mentioning at least twenty-seven names....This shows us that he had a considerable amount of knowledge, understanding, and care with regard to every one of them. Such recommendations and greetings show both the mutual concern among the saints and the mutual fellowship among the churches. It is by the churches' fellowship in the Body that the God of peace will crush Satan under our feet and we will be able to enjoy the rich grace of Christ. (*The Experience of God's Organic Salvation Equaling Reigning in Christ's Life,* pp. 67-70)

Further Reading: The Experience of God's Organic Salvation Equaling Reigning in Christ's Life, msg. 6; The Wonderful Christ in the Canon of the New Testament, ch. 10; The Practical Points concerning Blending, ch. 3

Enlightenment and inspiration: _____

_____

_____

Morning Nourishment

Matt. ...Moses, because of your hardness of heart, allowed
19:8 you,...but from the beginning it has not been so.
Eph. But holding to truth in love, we may grow up into
4:15-16 Him in all things, who is the Head, Christ, out from
whom all the Body...causes the growth of the Body
unto the building up of itself in love.

The words *recovery* and *economy* refer to one thing as seen from two viewpoints. With God, it is a matter of economy; with us, it is a matter of recovery. God's economy was unveiled through the apostles, but because the believers lost the proper understanding of God's economy, there is the need for it to be recovered. There- fore, what is being recovered today is God's economy. (*Life-study of 1 & 2 Samuel,* p. 195)

The Lord's recovery is the recovery of three main items. These items are vital for our practice of the church life, and it is crucial for us not to miss any of them.

First, the Lord's recovery is the recovery of the oneness of the Body of Christ. Throughout the past centuries, Christians have been divided again and again. In the eighteenth century, Count Zinzendorf saw the need of keeping the oneness of the Body of Christ, and a century later the Brethren in England saw more concerning the oneness of the Body and practiced it to some degree. Then in 1920 the Lord raised up Brother Watchman Nee in China and showed him the Body of Christ....From that time many young saints in China took the stand for the testimony of the oneness of the Body. The Lord's recovery is testifying that regardless of differing races, cultures, or levels of education, all Christians should be one. There is no reason for us to be divided. This is clearly revealed in the New Testament. (*The Basic Princi- ples for the Practice of the God-ordained Way,* pp. 1-2)

Today's Reading

Second, the Lord's recovery is the recovery, not of any doctrine, but of Christ as our all in all. Christ is everything. He is the center, and He is also the circumference. We only care for Christ.

Third, the Lord's recovery is the recovery of the function of all the members of the Body of Christ. The Lord desires that every member of His Body be a functioning member. Almost all Christian groups practice the system of the clergy and laity. The clergy are the professional preachers, pastors, and ministers, who serve God in place of the other members of the church. Actually, the clergy replaces the members of the Body of Christ, and this replacement spontaneously annuls and kills the function, the capacity, and the usefulness of the members of Christ. This is an offense to the Lord. The Lord's recovery is for the annulling of the clergy and laity and the developing of the gifts, functions, and capacity of all the members of the organic Body of Christ (Eph. 4:11-16).

The Lord has distributed talents to all of us [Matt. 25:14-30]. To some He gave five talents, to some He gave two talents, and to some He gave only one talent....The problem today is not with the five-talented ones, but with the one-talented ones....Not many churches have five-talented members, but they all have many one-talented members. Moreover, if we add together five one-talented members, they will equal a five-talented member.... Every member of the Body, regardless of how long he has been saved and how many talents he has received, must serve.

Brother Nee also pointed out to us that, according to 1 Corinthians 14, there is the need of the proper prophesying in order to build up the church as the organic Body of Christ. To prophesy is the best way to build up the Body. However, in most Christian meetings on the Lord's Day, there is a congregation with one or two speaking while the rest listen....After many years of meeting in this way, the functioning capacity and gifts of the members are spontaneously annulled. (*The Basic Principles for the Practice of the God-ordained Way,* pp. 2-4)

Further Reading: The Basic Principles for the Practice of the God-ordained Way; Life-study of 1 & 2 Samuel, msg. 30; *The Greatest Prophecy in the Bible,* ch. 2; *The High Peak of the Vision and the Reality of the Body of Christ,* ch. 1*

Enlightenment and inspiration: _____

_____
_____
_____

Morning Nourishment

Lev. ...Moses took some of its blood and put *it* on the
8:23 lobe of Aaron's right ear and on the thumb of his
right hand and on the big toe of his right foot.

[Leviticus 8:23-24a] signifies that the redeeming blood of Christ cleanses our ears, our hands, and our feet for the assuming of our New Testament priesthood. The service of the New Testament priesthood includes functioning in the meetings, preaching the gospel, and visiting the saints in their homes. For all these services, we need the cleansing of the blood of Christ.

Our moving (feet) and working (hands) are always under the direction of our hearing. We act according to what we hear. Therefore, in the church life, hearing is crucial.

By hearing we have been saved, and by hearing we may be nourished and edified. However, by hearing we may also be damaged and killed, and we may do evil things to others because of what we hear. Our hearing is a problem. In 2 Timothy 4:3 Paul speaks of those who "heap up to themselves teachers, having itching ears." Therefore, God's dealing must first touch the source—our hearing.

If any church would stop hearing negative things, that church would be very healthy and living. The church that is the weakest and the most deadened is the one full of criticism, gossip, and reasoning. (*Life-study of Leviticus*, p. 260)

Today's Reading

Since we are God's priests, we need to ask ourselves what kind of things we are willing to hear....Because we often hear unclean things, things that are unhealthy and contagious, we need to wash our ears with the blood of Christ. According to the Bible,... after the washing of the blood, we will enjoy the anointing of the Spirit. Then we will forget the negative things we heard, or at least we will not repeat these things. We will also become healthy and living, and the church will go on in our health.

Wherever we go, we need to take care of our hearing. If we do this, whatever we hear will be right and positive. Then we will go the right way and do the right work. However, if we do not take

care of our hearing but give ear to negative speaking, our deeds
and work will be affected in a negative way.

The purpose of the consecration offering (Lev. 8:23) is not to
deal with our sin and trespasses but to deal particularly with our
ear, our thumb, and our toe, that is, with our listening, our working, and our acting. If we are not careful about our ears,...instead
of ministering Christ, we will spread death. Today some devote
themselves to spreading death and not to spreading Christ, the
truth, and the gospel. Our listening ear, our working hand, and
our walking toe must be redeemed by the blood of Christ. We
must let the blood of Christ release us from all the negative
things. Then all the positive things of Christ will fill our hands.

Our hearing is mentioned first because it affects our working
and our moving. The blood of Christ deals with our ear for listening
...to God's speaking. To serve God as priests, we should be faithful
slaves...to God. As Isaiah 50:4 and 5 indicate, a servant must
have a hearing ear. A servant who does not listen to his master's
word cannot serve him according to his will, heart, and desire.

The cleansing of the right ear, the right thumb, and the big toe
of the right foot was needed on two occasions: at the ordination of
the priests and at the time of the cleansing of a leper (Lev. 14:14).
Both the lepers and the priests needed to have their ear, thumb,
and toe cleansed with the redeeming blood. This indicates that in
the eyes of God we sinners who have been ordained as God's
priests are lepers. As God's priests, His servants, we need to have
our ears redeemed from listening to anything other than God and
have them brought back to listening to the word of God. Also, we
need to have our working hand redeemed from doing anything
other than God's work. Furthermore, our toe for walking also
needs to be redeemed. (*Life-study of Leviticus,* pp. 261, 265-267)

Further Reading: Life-study of Leviticus, msgs. 22, 29-30; *The
    Training and the Practice of the Vital Groups,* msg. 1; *The Nor-
    mal Way of Fruit-bearing and Shepherding for the Building Up
    of the Church,* chs. 1, 3

Enlightenment and inspiration: _____
_____
_____
_____

Morning Nourishment

Lev. No meal offering that you present to Jehovah shall be 2:11 made with leaven, for you shall not burn any leaven or any honey as an offering by fire to Jehovah.

There is no leaven in the meal offering (Lev. 2:4-5, 11)....No leaven signifies that there is no sin or any negative thing in Christ (1 Cor. 5:6-8)....In the meal offering there is no honey, which will ferment (Lev. 2:11). This signifies that there is no natural affection or natural good in Christ.

Two things in the Lord's recovery bother me. One is ambition, which I regard as leaven. The other is natural affection, which I regard as honey. Certain saints may claim that their love for one another is according to the Lord's commandment (John 13:34). Actually, their love is a matter of natural affection and has nothing to do with the Lord's commandment.

Nothing damages the church life, the Lord's ministry, and the Lord's work more than ambition and natural affection. Ambition for leadership is leaven, and leaven brings in corruption. Natural affection is honey, and honey brings in rottenness.

Ambition and affection are closely related. Suppose a brother has a particular ambition. If his ambition is fulfilled, he will be happy. If it is not fulfilled, he will be unhappy. He will love anyone who helps him to gain what he desires. But anyone who hinders him in fulfilling his ambition will be regarded as an enemy.

If we want to serve the Lord for a long period of time, we must look to the Lord to purify us from ambition and natural affection. No matter how well certain saints may treat us, and no matter how close we are or how long we have been together, we should not make friends in the church life. Rather, we should regard all the saints in the same way—as brothers and sisters in the Lord. We should not be ambitious, and we should not have natural affection, for such affection will bring in rottenness.

The meal offering must have neither leaven nor honey. We should take Christ as fine flour without adding leaven or honey. We need to ask the Lord to purify us so that in our living there will be no leaven and no honey. (*Life-study of Leviticus*, pp. 115-116)

Today's Reading

Discernment in diet is a matter...of discernment in what we eat. ...Leviticus is a book of types, and in types there are figures which bear a particular significance. The significance is different from the thing itself. This is true of the animals mentioned in Leviticus 11. All these animals bear a great significance, for...they are figures that describe different kinds of persons. This is proved by Acts 10:9b-14, 27-29....Eventually [Peter] came to understand [that the animals, reptiles, and birds in his vision were figures of people].

To eat is to contact the things outside of us that could affect us inside. This especially refers to our contacting of people. When we eat we contact something that is outside of us, something that has nothing to do with us. However, if we eat that thing, it can affect us inside. In Leviticus 11 the things we eat signify people, and eating signifies our contacting of people.

To eat is not merely to contact something but also to receive something into us....We all are a constitution of the food we eat and digest. Eventually, what we digest becomes us; it becomes our very constitution. This indicates that contacting people is an important matter. If we intend to live a holy life as required by the holy God, we need to be careful about our contact with people. Our contact with certain kinds of people can cause us to be reconstituted and thus make us another kind of person. Whatever we contact we will receive, and whatever we receive will reconstitute us, making us a different kind of person from what we are now.

We all must learn to be careful and cautious in contacting people....When we are about to have contact with a particular person, we need to consider whether he is clean or unclean. Such a consideration will preserve us and keep us from being defiled or corrupted. (*Life-study of Leviticus,* pp. 313-314, 319)

Further Reading: Life-study of Leviticus, msgs. 13, 36-37; *The Ministry of the New Testament and the Teaching and Fellowship of the Apostles,* ch. 2

Enlightenment and inspiration: _____

_____

_____

_____

Hymns, #539

1 O Lord, Thou art in me as life
    And everything to me!
Subjective and available,
    Thus I experience Thee.

    O Lord, Thou art the Spirit!
      How dear and near to me!
    How I admire Thy marvelous
      Availability!

2 To all my needs both great and small
    Thou art the rich supply;
So ready and sufficient too
    For me now to apply.

3 Thy sweet anointing with Thy might
    In weakness doth sustain;
By Thy supply of energy
    My strength Thou dost maintain.

4 Thy law of life in heart and mind
    My conduct regulates;
The wealth of Thy reality
    My being saturates.

5 O Thou art ever one with me,
    Unrivaled unity!
One spirit with me all the time
    For all eternity!

Composition for prophecy with main point and sub-points: _____

WEEK 2 — OUTLINE 22

Knowing the Present Truth,
Upholding the Absoluteness of the Truth,
and Being Constituted with the Truth
for the Church as the Pillar and Base of the Truth

Scripture Reading: John 18:37; 1 Tim. 2:4; 2 Pet. 1:12; 2 John 1-2; 3 John 3; 1 Tim. 3:15-16

Day 1 I. **The Lord's recovery is the recovery of the divine truths as revealed in the Word of God (John 8:32):**

A. The truths in the Word have been lost, misunderstood, and wrongly applied; thus, there is the need of the Lord's recovery (2 Tim. 2:15).

B. The truths in the Bible have both the objective aspect and the subjective aspect; the objective doctrines are for the subjective truths, and the subjective truths are for the producing of the church (2 John 1-2, 4; 3 John 3-4, 8).

C. The recovery has the highest truth—the truth that is the consummation of the truths recovered during the past centuries (2 Tim. 2:2, 15).

D. The standard of the Lord's recovery depends on the standard of the truth we put out (1 Tim. 2:4; 2 Tim. 2:15; Titus 1:1).

Day 2 II. **We need to know the present truth, the up-to-date truth (2 Pet. 1:12):**

A. Every worker of the Lord should inquire before God as to what the present truth is (John 8:32; 3 John 8):

1. During particular periods of time God releases certain truths and causes them to be revealed once more.

2. Although there are many major and crucial truths in the Bible, what we need to know is God's present truth, His up-to-date truth (2 Pet. 1:12).

B. In the recovery the light of the truth is up to date (John 8:12, 32; 1 John 1:5-6).

C. We need to release the truth that God became man so that man may become God in life and nature but not in the Godhead, and the truth concerning the New Jerusalem (Rom. 8:3; 1:3-4; John 1:12-14; Rev. 21:2, 9-11):

1. The New Jerusalem is a composition of God's chosen, redeemed, regenerated, sanctified, transformed, and glorified people who have been deified (vv. 2, 9-11):

   a. On God's side, the Triune God was incarnated to be a man (John 1:14).

   b. On our side, we are being deified, constituted with the processed and consummated Triune God so that we may be made God in life and in nature to be His corporate expression for eternity (Rev. 21:2, 9-11).

2. In Christ God has become man to make man God in life and nature but not in the Godhead so that the redeeming God and the redeemed man can be mingled, constituted, and incorporated together to become one entity—the New Jerusalem; this is the highest truth (John 1:12-14; 14:20; Rev. 21:2).

Day 3 III. **The truth is always absolute, and God wants us to uphold the absoluteness of the truth (John 14:6; 18:37; 3 John 3-4, 8):**

A. Every worker of the Lord must uphold the absoluteness of the truth (v. 8).

B. Being absolute for the truth means that no personal feelings or relationships are allowed to stand in the way of the truth (John 14:6; Matt. 10:37-39).

C. Because the truth is absolute, we have to sacrifice ourselves and put ourselves aside (16:24; Rev. 2:13; 12:11b).

D. We must stand on the side of the truth to oppose ourselves; only in this way can we maintain the truth and not ourselves (John 18:37; Rev. 1:5a).

E. We are here to follow the truth, not man, and we are here to maintain the absoluteness of the truth (Rom. 3:4; 2 Tim. 2:15, 25; Titus 1:1).

Day 4 **IV. We need to be constituted with the truth (1 John 1:8; 2:4; 2 John 1-2):**

A. We must come to the full knowledge of the truth—a thorough apprehension of the truth, a full acknowledgement and appreciation of the reality of the spiritual and divine things (1 Tim. 2:4).

B. The best way to learn the divine truths is to study the translated and properly interpreted Holy Scriptures (2 Tim. 3:14-17; Prov. 23:23):

1. The best help in seeing the intrinsic significance of the word of the Bible is the Recovery Version with the footnotes and the Life-studies (Neh. 8:8, 13).

2. We need to study the messages on the high peak of the divine revelation (1994-1997) and learn to speak the high-peak truths according to the new language of the new culture in the divine and mystical realm (1 Cor. 2:13).

Day 5 C. To be constituted with the truth is to have the intrinsic element of the divine revelation wrought into us to become our organic constitution (Psa. 51:6):

1. The intrinsic element of the divine revelation must be wrought into and constituted into our being (Col. 3:16; 1 John 1:8; 2:4; 2 John 2).

2. Once the truth enters into us through our understanding and remains in our memory, we will have an accumulation of the truth, and the truth will become a constant and long-term nourishment (vv. 1-2).

Day 6 **V. The church is the supporting pillar and the holding base of the truth (1 Tim. 3:15-16):**

A. *Truth* in 1 Timothy 3:15 refers to the real things

in the New Testament concerning Christ and
the church according to God's New Testament
economy (Matt. 16:16, 18; Eph. 5:32).

B. The truth is the Triune God, having Christ as
the embodiment, center, and expression, to produce the church as the Body of Christ, the house
of God, and the kingdom of God (Col. 2:9; Eph.
1:22-23; 4:16; 1 Tim. 3:15; John 3:3, 5).

C. In particular, "the truth" in 1 Timothy 3:15
refers to "He who was manifested in the flesh"
in verse 16:

1. Here *truth* refers to God entering into man
and being manifested in man; thus, the
truth is God manifested in the flesh.

2. The church is the pillar and base of the
truth of God being manifested in the flesh;
the church upholds and presents to the universe the fact of God's manifestation in the
flesh.

VI. In the Lord's recovery we must take "the
way of the truth"—the path of the Christian
life according to the truth, which is the reality of the contents of the New Testament
(2 Pet. 2:2).

Morning Nourishment

John   And you shall know the truth, and the truth shall
8:32   set you free.
2 Tim. Be diligent to present yourself approved to God, an
2:15   unashamed workman, cutting straight the word of
       the truth.
3 John For I rejoiced greatly at the brothers' coming and
3   testifying to your *steadfastness in the* truth, even as
       you walk in truth.

Today the whole earth needs the truth of the Lord that is in His Word. Regrettably, however, the Bible, the divine Word, has not been fully opened to the world. Thus, it has not been possible for people to fully know the truth of the Lord. At the most, Christians are able to boast that the holy Word of God has been published into many languages and propagated over the whole earth. Yet they are not able to say that after reading the Bible, regardless of which language, they have been able to truly understand the deep mysteries within it.

The truths in the holy Word of the Lord were completed approximately two thousand years ago, but over a period of a little more than one thousand years they seemed to slowly vanish. Only in the last few centuries have the truths again been released little by little through the zealous and careful study of many lovers of the Lord. This is what we refer to as the Lord's recovery. The Lord's recovery is the recovery of all the truths in the Bible that were lost. Thus, the recovery of the truth is one of the great pillars in the Lord's recovery. The Lord's recovery lies with the recovery of the knowledge of the truth. (*Truth, Life, the Church, and the Gospel—the Four Great Pillars in the Lord's Recovery,* pp. 43-44)

Today's Reading

The truths in the Holy Scriptures are always of two aspects: the objective aspect and the subjective aspect. We have to be clear that all the objective doctrines are for the subjective experience. If we pay attention only to the objective doctrines and neglect the subjective aspect, we will not be able to fulfill God's eternal purpose, which is the church. The objective doctrines are for the subjective truths, and the subjective truths are for the producing of the church....When we have the experience of the subjective truths, the church is spontaneously produced.

Furthermore, all the subjective truths are linked to the Spirit and life. The Spirit and life are the substance of the subjective truths....Objective doctrines are composed of letters, whereas subjective truths are constituted with the Spirit and life....Therefore, it is by the Spirit and life that the church is produced. Because we live by the Spirit and in life, we have the experience of the subjective truths and therefore have the church life. (*The Subjective Truths in the Holy Scriptures*, pp. 21-22)

I feel that for the long range for the Lord's recovery in such a top country as the United States, which is full of culture, education, scientific knowledge, and biblical knowledge, the greatest need we must meet is to bring the saints in the Lord's recovery into the truth to carry the Lord's recovery on. For a country to be strong there is the need to bring its people into the proper education. If the people are behind in education, that country is also behind. The reason why the United States is a top country is because of its highest education.

Today we are here for the Lord's recovery. For the long run, we surely have to help the saints in the Lord's recovery to get into the top spiritual education. You must remember that we still uplift the living Christ, the life-giving Spirit, life itself and its riches, and the church in a living way. To promote these things, to carry these things out, and to bring people into these things so that they remain there, we need the Word and we need the truth. The standard of the Lord's recovery depends upon the standard of the truth we put out. The truths will be the measure and the standard. (*Elders' Training, Book 3: The Way to Carry Out the Vision*, p. 102)

Further Reading: Truth, Life, the Church, and the Gospel—the Four Great Pillars in the Lord's Recovery, ch. 4; *The Subjective Truths in the Holy Scriptures*, chs. 3-4

Enlightenment and inspiration: _____
_____
_____
_____

Morning Nourishment

**2 Pet. Therefore I will be ready always to remind you con-
1:12 cerning these things, even though you know *them*
and have been established in the present truth.
3 John I have no greater joy than these things, that I hear
4 that my children are walking in the truth.
8 We therefore ought to support such ones that we
may become fellow workers in the truth.
Rev. And I saw the holy city, New Jerusalem, coming down
21:2 out of heaven from God, prepared as a bride adorned
for her husband.**

Second Peter 1:12 mentions the words *established in the present truth. The present truth* can also be rendered *the up-to-date truth.* What is the up-to-date truth?...Although [all the truths are] in the Bible, through man's foolishness, unfaithfulness, negligence, and disobedience many of the truths were lost and hidden from man.... Not until the fullness of time did God release certain truths during particular periods of time and cause them to be revealed once more.

These freshly revealed truths are not God's new inventions. Rather, they are man's new discoveries. There is no need for invention, but there is the need for discovery. In past generations God revealed different truths. During certain periods of time, He caused men to discover these specific truths. We can see this clearly from the history of the church. (Watchman Nee, *What Are We?*, pp. 2-3)

Today's Reading

[Martin Luther] was a vessel raised up by God to unveil the truth of justification by faith. This does not mean that before Luther there was no such thing as justification by faith. The fact already existed....Luther was merely the one who realized this truth in a stronger way; he was particularly outstanding in this truth. For this reason, this truth became the "present truth" in that age.

Every worker of the Lord should inquire before God as to what the present truth is....Although there are many major and crucial truths in the Bible, what we need to know is God's present truth. Not only do we need to know the general truths, we must also be clear about God's present truth.

The truth of justification by faith was definitely recovered. God dug up this buried truth from all the traditions, human opinions, and creeds and caused this truth to be known and preached once more. If a person were born in that age, what he should have done was preach this truth and exhort others concerning this truth. If he did not do this, he should not be considered a faithful worker of God in that age. (Watchman Nee, *What Are We?*, pp. 3-4, 6)

The main contents of the New Testament are that the Triune God has an eternal economy according to His good pleasure to dispense Himself into His chosen and redeemed people in His life and in His nature, to make all of them the same as He is in life and nature, to make them His duplication that they may express Him. This corporate expression will consummate in the New Jerusalem. Thus, the New Jerusalem is simply the enlarged, the increased, incarnation consummated in full, that is, the fullness of the Triune God for Him to express Himself in His divinity mingled with humanity.

In our spiritual breathing by the exercise of our spirit, we enjoy, receive, and absorb the divine substance with the divine essence, the divine element, and the divine expression. This will cause us to be deified, that is, to be constituted with the processed Triune God to made God in life and in nature but not in the Godhead. In this sense we may speak of the deification of the believers, a process that will consummate in the New Jerusalem.

The New Jerusalem is a composition of God's chosen, redeemed, regenerated, sanctified, transformed, and glorified people who have been deified. On God's side, the Triune God has been incarnated to be a man; on our side, we are being deified, constituted with the processed and consummated Triune God so that we may be made God in life and in nature to be His corporate expression for eternity. This is the highest truth, and this is the highest gospel. (*Life-study of Job*, pp. 64, 122)

Further Reading: What Are We?; Life-study of Job, msgs. 10, 16, 22

Enlightenment and inspiration: _____

_____

_____

_____

Morning Nourishment

John **Jesus said to him, I am the way and the reality and the**
14:6 **life; no one comes to the Father except through Me.**
18:37 **...For this I have been born, and for this I have come**
into the world, that I would testify to the truth. Every-
one who is of the truth hears My voice.
2 Tim. **In meekness correcting those who oppose, if perhaps**
2:25 **God may give them repentance unto the full knowl-**
edge of the truth.

Every worker of the Lord must uphold the absoluteness of the truth. This is possible only when a man is delivered from himself. Many brothers and sisters are not absolute to the truth; they are affected by people, things, and personal feelings. If a man is not absolute to the truth, he will, in the course of his work, sacrifice God's truth for man, himself, or his own desires. A basic requirement for being a servant of the Lord is to not sacrifice the truth. We can sacrifice ourselves and our desires, but we can never sacrifice the truth. The problems with many workers stem from the relationship with their friends, intimate acquaintances, and family. The truth is compromised...[because of these relationships]. God cannot use such people. If the truth is the truth, it should not be compromised. (Watchman Nee, *The Character of the Lord's Worker,* p. 151)

Today's Reading

The standard of the divine Word must not be lowered to the level of our personal attainment. We cannot tamper with the truth in any way in order to justify our own deficiencies. This is what it means to be absolute to the truth. We have to transcend ourselves, our own feelings, and our own personal interest in our speaking. This is a high requirement for the servants of the Lord. We must beware of doing things one way as they affect other brothers and sisters but doing them another way as they are applied to our spouse or our children. The truth is always absolute. God wants us to uphold the absoluteness of the truth. If God's Word says something, it is so, no matter who is involved. We cannot make exceptions just because of some special relationships. If we do, we are lowering the standard of God's truth.

We have to see the glory of God's truth. We cannot project our own feelings into His truth. When we stand beside God's truth, we should not just consider ourselves to be smaller than it; we should consider ourselves to be non-existent. If we involve the self even a little, we will end up with trouble immediately.

To be absolute to the truth...means to set aside feelings, to ignore personal relationships, and to not stand for the self. The truth is absolute. Our personal feelings, relationships, experiences, and encounters should not be mixed up with it. Since truth is absolute, what is right is right and what is wrong is wrong.

It is not a small thing to be absolute to the truth. We cannot be indifferent about this. If we are loose in this, we will be loose in everything. In order to uphold the truth, we have to abandon ourselves completely. If we do not have such a heart and habit for the truth, we will have problems sooner or later.

Let us deal with this matter conscientiously before the Lord. It is a very crucial and serious matter. Let us remember that there is no place whatsoever for personal feelings and sentiments in the work of the Lord. Even if our personal sentiments can positively influence others to receive the truth, we should still keep them out of the work. We may influence a person to receive the truth by inviting him for dinner, but this is wrong. Truth is absolute. Out of the goodness of our hearts we may want to do something to uphold the truth, but truth requires no human hand to uphold it. It has its own standing, its own authority, and its own power, and it needs no human hand to uphold it. We do not have to lend truth a helping hand. We should not be afraid of anyone's rejection of the truth. We only need to learn to honor God's truth, to take the way of the truth, and to not compromise the truth in any way. (Watchman Nee, *The Character of the Lord's Worker,* pp. 152-155, 158)

Further Reading: The Character of the Lord's Worker, ch. 10; *Truth, Life, the Church, and the Gospel—the Four Great Pillars in the Lord's Recovery,* ch. 5

Enlightenment and inspiration: _____

_____
_____
_____

Morning Nourishment

1 Tim. This is good and acceptable in the sight of our Savior
2:3-4 God, who desires all men to be saved and to come to
the full knowledge of the truth.
Prov. Buy truth, and do not sell *it;* / *Buy* wisdom and
23:23 instruction and understanding.
Psa. The opening of Your words gives light, / Imparting
119:130 understanding to the simple.

[According to 1 Timothy 2:4], we should pray on behalf of all
men because God our Savior desires all men to be saved and
know the truth. Our prayer is required for the carrying out of
God's desire. God desires all men not only to be saved, but also to
have the full knowledge of the truth. Truth means reality, denoting all the real things revealed in God's Word, which are mainly
Christ as the embodiment of God and the church as the Body of
Christ. Every saved person should have a full knowledge, a complete realization, of these things. (*Life-study of 1 Timothy,* p. 29)

Today's Reading

Up to the present time it has been fully proven among us that
the most profitable writings and publications are the Life-study
messages with the notes of the Recovery Version. I wrote these
things, not for scholarly study for people to get a degree, but for
life ministering, for truth releasing, and for opening up the books
of the Bible....We are not for theology, but we are for "theos," God.
Our publications are not for any kind of "ology," but just for God,
the Triune God, the processed Triune God, and the Lord, Christ,
Jesus, the Spirit, life, and the church. Our publications are for a
living person....I do have a burden to publish things full of Christ,
full of the triune, processed God, full of the life-giving Spirit, full of
life, and full of the church. The Lord's recovery is just for the
recovery of the processed Triune God to be dispensed into us, and
the living Christ, the Spirit, life, and the church are the crucial
contents of the Lord's recovery. There is no other place to pick up
books which are so rich, so enlightening, and so nourishing concerning the recovery of Christ, the Spirit, life, and the church.

Since this is the real situation and the real condition, I feel that we have no choice but to use the Life-studies, because we realize that this is the best way to bring people into the holy Word.

The holy Word itself says in Psalm 119:130: "The opening of Your words gives light." Millions of copies of the Bible have been distributed. They have been placed in hotels, in homes, and in many places. Nearly everywhere you go today you find a Bible, but who has entered into the Bible? There has nearly been no entrance. Many have a copy of the Bible, but the Bible has been closed and nearly never opened. Now the Lord has given us a key, an opener. I consider our writings as the opener to open the holy Word. I believe that those of you who have read the Life-study messages can testify honestly that these messages with the notes of the Recovery Version have opened up a certain chapter or a certain book of the Bible to you. This is not to replace the Bible, but to bring people into the Bible. (*Elders' Training, Book 3: The Way to Carry Out the Vision,* pp. 101-102)

Christians today are shallow because they would not pay the price to labor adequately. These riches are all here in the Bible, just like gold in a mine, but nearly no one would labor to dig them out....I hope, brothers, that in your localities you would not repeat the old things. We should learn to go on, to learn the things in the heavenlies, and to learn to speak these higher and deeper things. ...This will require your time. To dig out the gold is not that easy. I would encourage all of us to go on in this way. Otherwise, the Lord would not have much of a way to go on; we will delay Him, retain Him, hold Him back. Some of us even repeat the things we taught twenty-three years ago. What we are teaching holds people back....We should go further. Let us go on. There is real hope for us to go on in His recovery. (*Elders' Training, Book 5: Fellowship concerning the Lord's Up-to-date Move,* p. 55)

Further Reading: Elders' Training, Book 3: The Way to Carry Out the Vision, ch. 10; Elders' Training, Book 5: Fellowship concerning the Lord's Up-to-date Move, ch. 3

Enlightenment and inspiration: _____

_____

_____

_____

Morning Nourishment

Psa. Behold, You delight in truth in the inward parts; /
51:6 And in the hidden *part* You would make known
wisdom to me.

Col. Let the word of Christ dwell in you richly in all
3:16 wisdom, teaching and admonishing one another
with psalms *and* hymns *and* spiritual songs, singing with grace in your hearts to God.

If we continue to take our old way, I am afraid that after
another ten years we will be in the same condition. We are just
giving people a little injection to help them grow in life mainly by
inspiration, but no solid truth has been constituted into their
being that can remain in their memory and that can be presented
to others in a proper doctrinal way. By taking the way we have
taken, we have lost the nature of the testimony of Jesus which
must be a constitution of the proper truth that produces a proper
daily living. If the saints are not properly constituted with the
truth, they cannot live a proper life. If they only live by inspiration
and not by the constitution of the truth, I do not trust in that kind
of living to be a testimony of the Lord. (*Elders' Training, Book 3:
The Way to Carry Out the Vision,* p. 139)

Today's Reading

Just for us to meet properly, to stand on the unique ground,
and to have a so-called church life without such a prevailing testimony shining out from within us would not make the Lord happy
concerning His recovery. We must give the Lord a way to have a
recovery full of life and full of the knowledge of the truth so that
we can be those preaching the gospel, teaching the truth, and
ministering life. If we become constituted with the truth, when we
open up our mouth our preaching will be rich. It will not be rich
in stories, jokes, or even in so-called biblical doctrines, but rich in
Christ, in the Spirit, in life, and in the church. We do have the way
to carry this out, because we have the Word. The Word is the con-
veyer which conveys the gospel, the truth, and life. (*Elders' Training, Book 3: The Way to Carry Out the Vision,* p. 144)

If we do not have the knowledge, we cannot have the experience or the enjoyment. If we do not have the experience and enjoyment of Christ, we simply cannot gain Christ. Then when we go to speak to others, we will have nothing to say and will be poor in utterance and void of words.

Some co-workers and elders often would say to me, "I don't dare to speak about these high truths because the believers whom I am serving cannot understand them according to their present spiritual condition." My reply is: "It is not that they cannot understand, but it is that you cannot speak clearly." It is only after we have known, experienced, and gained Christ that we can speak to others, according to the new language in the Lord's recovery, concerning this Christ whom we have gained. We must learn to use the new language to speak the new culture in the divine and mystical realm. Then people will listen to us with great pleasure and will definitely understand the things we speak. (*How to Be a Co-worker and an Elder and How to Fulfill Their Obligations,* pp. 16-17)

If you merely read the Life-studies, you will only receive a temporary nourishment. That will only become a kind of inspiration to you. An inspiration is like a vapor in the air. When what we read becomes a truth in our being, this nourishment remains forever....What I have received from the Lord is always the solid truth, so it remains in me, nourishing me all the time. You must have the truth....The truth gets into you through your mentality, your understanding....If the truth gets into your memory, it becomes a constant and long-term nourishment. Then you have an accumulation of the truth, and you are a person continually under the constant nourishment. You will then know how to present the truth to others, not merely to inspire them or to stir them up, but to make them solid and constituted with the truth. (*Elders' Training, Book 3: The Way to Carry Out the Vision,* p. 93)

Further Reading: Elders' Training, Book 3: The Way to Carry Out the Vision, chs. 9, 13; *How to Be a Co-worker and an Elder and How to Fulfill Their Obligations,* ch. 1

Enlightenment and inspiration: _____

_____

_____

_____

Morning Nourishment

1 Tim.   But if I delay, *I write* that you may know how one
3:15-16   ought to conduct himself in <u>the house of God</u>, which is
          <u>the church of the living God, the pillar and base of the</u>
          <u>truth.</u> And confessedly, great is the mystery of godli-
          ness: <u>He who was manifested in the flesh,</u> / Justified
          in the Spirit, / Seen by angels, / Preached among the
          nations, / Believed on in the world, / Taken up in glory.
2 Pet.   And many will follow their licentiousness, because of
2:2   whom <u>the way of the truth</u> will be reviled.

In 1 Timothy 3:15 Paul tells us that the church as the house of
the living God is "the pillar and base of the truth." The church is
the supporting pillar and holding base of the truth. Here truth
refers to the real things revealed in the New Testament concerning Christ and the church according to God's New Testament
economy. The church is the supporting pillar and holding base of
these realities. A local church should be such a building that
holds, bears, and testifies the truth, the reality, of Christ and the
church. (*The Conclusion of the New Testament,* p. 2232)

Today's Reading

According to 1 Timothy 3:15…the church is the house of the
living God; the church is also the pillar and base of the truth.…
The truth spoken of in this verse is "He who was manifested in
the flesh" in [verse 16].

<u>Truth is God being manifested in man; the joining of God and</u>
<u>man is truth.</u>…We should not say that God is truth; rather, <u>God</u>
<u>becoming flesh and entering into man is truth,</u> because without
God being added, all the created things are false and empty.…Only
when electricity enters into the electric lamp can it be real and
true. God is the reality of all things, just as electricity is the reality
of the electric lamp. Electricity itself does not need to become real,
because it is real. Likewise, our spirit and soul are the reality of
our body as a shell; if our spirit and soul leave, our body becomes a
sham. God must enter into human beings so that they may have
the reality in them. Hence, truth refers to God's entering into

man, that is, the Creator's entering into His creatures. This is called truth, which is the manifestation of God in the flesh.

The truth of God being manifested in the flesh is upheld by the church. The church is the pillar and the base of this truth. The church is too great; God manifested in the flesh is a great matter. The Bible says, "Great is the mystery of godliness" (1 Tim. 3:16). This great matter is upheld by the church. The church is the pillar and base of God being manifested in the flesh, and this matter needs to be upheld by the church. When we see the church, we see the manifestation of God in the flesh. If the church is not present, the manifestation of God is finished.

This reminds us of what the Lord Jesus said in Matthew 16:18: "Upon this rock I will build My church." We all know that Christ is the rock, the foundation, upon which the church is built. When we come to 1 Timothy, however, we see that the church becomes the base of God's manifestation in the flesh. The fact of this mystery rests with the church. The church is the pillar and base of this matter. A pillar denotes support, which can be seen in the beams of a house which are supported by pillars. However, with regard to the truth of God being manifested in the flesh, the church is not only the pillar but also the base. This shows that the church upholds and presents the matter of God's manifestation in the flesh to the universe in time and space. God entrusts this mystery to the church.

All who serve God in the church...must be brought by the Lord to such a high realm to see that the church is the pillar and base of the truth, upholding the fact of God's manifestation in the universe. This is a great and mysterious matter. Without this vision, we will not know what we are doing. A day must come when our eyes are opened to see that the church we serve and administrate is such a great matter; only then will we know what we are doing. (*How to Administrate the Church*, pp. 13-15)

Further Reading: The Conclusion of the New Testament, msg. 208; *How to Administrate the Church*, ch. 1

Enlightenment and inspiration: _____

_____

_____

_____

Hymns, #804

1   Thy Word is like a storehouse, Lord,
     With full provision there,
And everyone who seeks may come,
     Its glorious wealth to share.
Thy Word is like a deep, deep mine,
     And jewels rich and rare
Are hidden in its mighty depths
     For every searcher there.

2   Thy Word is like a starry host:
     A thousand rays of light
Are seen to guide the traveler,
     And make his pathway bright.
Thy Word is like an armory,
     Where soldiers may repair,
And find, for life's long battle day,
     All needful weapons there.

3   O may I love Thy precious Word,
     May I explore the mine,
May I its glorious riches take,
     May light upon me shine.
O may I find my armor there,
     Thy Word my trusty sword;
I'll learn to fight with every foe
     The battle of the Lord.

4   Word of the ever living God,
     Will of His glorious Son;
Without Thee how could earth be trod,
     Or God and Christ be won?
Lord, grant us all aright to learn
     The wisdom it imparts,
And to its heav'nly teaching turn,
     With simple, child-like hearts.

Composition for prophecy with main point and sub-points: _____

_____
_____
_____
_____
_____
_____
_____
_____
_____
_____
_____
_____
_____
_____
_____
_____
_____
_____
_____
_____
_____
_____
_____
_____
_____
_____
_____
_____
_____
_____
_____
_____
_____
_____

Caring for the Oneness of the Body of Christ by Seeing, Experiencing, and Applying Twelve Crucial Matters

Scripture Reading: John 17:11, 17, 21-23; Eph. 4:3-6

Day 1   I. The Lord's recovery is the recovery of the oneness of the Body of Christ (Eph. 4:3-4):
  A. The Lord's recovery is based upon the truth that Christ has only one Body (1 Cor. 12:12-13, 20; Eph. 1:23; 4:4, 16).
  B. The Lord desires to recover the Body of Christ and the oneness of the Body of Christ (v. 3; John 17:11, 21-22).
  C. The oneness of the Body of Christ is the oneness of the Spirit; therefore, we need to be diligent to keep the oneness of the Spirit (Eph. 4:3):
    1. For us to keep the oneness of the Spirit, we need to be dealt with by the cross (Rom. 6:6; Matt. 16:24).
    2. If we would keep the oneness of the Spirit, our flesh, our self, and our "I" must be crossed out by the cross of Christ (Gal. 2:20; 5:24).

  II. The one unique, universal Body of Christ is expressed as the local churches (Eph. 4:4; Rev. 1:4, 11):
  A. A local church is the expression of the Body of Christ in a certain locality (Matt. 16:18; 18:17; 1 Cor. 1:2; 10:32b; 12:12-13, 20, 27).
  B. The one universal church—the Body of Christ—becomes the many local churches—local expressions of the Body of Christ (Rom. 12:4-5; 16:16b).
  C. Every local church is part of the unique, universal Body of Christ and is a local expression of this Body (1 Cor. 1:2; 12:27).

Day 2 III. The ground of the church is constituted of three crucial elements:

Eph. 4.3-4 Be diligent to keep the oneness of the Spirit in the uniting bond of peace
One Body & one Spirit even as also you were called in one hope of your calling
one Lord

Acts 14:23 And when
they had appointed
for them elders in
every church

Titus 1:5 And appoint
elders in every city as
I directed you

Rev 1:11 Sent & to 7
churches, to Ephesus,...

1 John 5:6 the Spt is
the reality (of all that
Ca the Son is).

John 16:13 The Spt of reality
will guide you into all the
reality

A. The first element of the church ground is the unique oneness of the universal Body of Christ—"the oneness of the Spirit" (Eph. 4:3-4). *oneness of John 17*

B. The second element of the church ground is the unique ground of the locality in which a local church is established and exists (Acts 14:23; Titus 1:5; Rev. 1:11). *absolute prerequisite for maintaining proper order in a local church*

 ＊ C. The third element of the church ground is the reality of the Spirit of oneness, expressing the unique oneness of the universal Body of Christ on the unique ground of locality as a local church (1 John 5:6; John 16:13):

 1. By the Spirit of reality, who is the living reality of the Divine Trinity, the oneness of the Body of Christ becomes real and living.

 2. Through this Spirit the ground of the church is applied in life and not in legality.

4

IV. **The ground of oneness is the processed and consummated Triune God applied to our being (17:21-22; 2 Cor. 13:14; Eph. 3:14-17a; 4:4-6):**

A. The oneness of the Body of Christ is actually the triune, organic, living God Himself (1:3-14, 22-23; 3:14-17a; 4:4-6):

 1. Ephesians 4:4-6 reveals four persons—one Body, one Spirit, one Lord, and one God and Father—mingled together as one entity to be the organic Body of Christ.

 2. The church is the Triune God mingled with His redeemed people to become the golden lampstand to express God (Rev. 1:20).

B. We have been brought into the oneness produced by the application of the processed and consummated Triune God to our being (John 17:21-22; 2 Cor. 13:14).

C. The oneness in the churches in the Lord's recovery involves the application of the Triune God to our inner being (Eph. 3:14-17a).

Jn 8:12 I am the light of the world; if anyone comes after me, he will have the light of life
10:10 I came that they may have life and may have it abundantly
11:25 I am the resurrection & the life; he who believes into Me, even if he sld die, shall live
WEEK 3 — OUTLINE 42

Day 3 5 **V. The essence of oneness is life and light (John 8:12; 10:10; 11:25):**

A. The oneness is in life, with light, and on the proper ground (Psa. 36:8-9).

B. The Father's name is a matter of life, and the Father's truth is a matter of light (John 17:11, 17):

1. Without life, there can be no oneness (Ezek. 37:1-14); the only way oneness can be maintained is by life, in life, and with life (Gen. 2:9; Rev. 22:1-2).

2. Divisiveness and divisions are the issue of taking into our being something other than life (Gen. 3:1-6; 11:1-9).

3. Light preserves oneness and rules out disorder (Rev. 21:23).

C. Light, life, and oneness go together and are a cycle: the more light, the more life; the more life, the more oneness; and the more oneness, the more light.

D. All the churches in the Lord's recovery must be in life and under the shining of light (1 John 1:1-5); by the shining of light and by the watering and supplying of life, we are one (Rev. 21:23; 22:1-2).

VI. There are six tests of a genuine local church (1:4, 11):

A. A genuine local church has no special name (3:8).

B. A genuine local church has no special teaching or practice (Acts 2:42).

C. A genuine local church has no special fellowship (1 Cor. 1:9).

D. A genuine local church has no separate administration.

E. A genuine local church has no hidden connection with other organizations.

F. A genuine local church is willing to have fellowship with all the local churches (10:16-17; 16:19; 1 Thes. 2:14; Rev. 1:4; 2:7a).

Day 4 **VII. The damage to the oneness of God's people is portrayed in the Old Testament:**
- A. Joshua 22:10-34 shows us that no matter what the situation of God's people might be today, we are not allowed to set up another altar for the worship of God and for fellowship with God.
- B. The significance of the high places is division and involves the exaltation of something (1 Kings 11:6-8; 13:33-34; 14:22-24; 15:14, 34; 22:43):
  1. In principle, every "high place," every division, involves the uplifting, the exaltation, of something other than Christ (1 Cor. 1:10-13).
  2. In the church life we should not have any "high places"; instead, we should all be on one level to exalt Christ (Col. 1:18; 3:10-11).
- C. Jeroboam's apostasy broke God's ordination of having one unique worship center in the holy land for the keeping of the oneness of the children of Israel (1 Kings 12:25-33).

VIII. The truth sanctifies us for oneness (John 17:17):
- A. The truth sanctifies, and sanctification issues in oneness (vv. 21-22).
- B. To be sanctified is to move out of ourselves and into the Triune God and to allow Christ to live in us (vv. 11, 14-17, 21-26).
- C. The four factors of division—worldliness, ambition, self-exaltation, and opinions and concepts—can be dealt with only by the sanctifying truth (v. 17).

Day 5 **IX. The genuine oneness is versus "the evil" (vv. 15-17, 21-23):**
- A. The world is the satanic system with Satan as the evil within it; Satan and the world are one entity (vv. 14-16).
- B. The evil (v. 15) is the world with its ambition, self-exaltation, and opinions and concepts, all of which produce division.

C. In the Triune God there is no ambition, in the glory of the Father there is no self-exaltation, and in the place where Christ lives and reigns there are no opinions and concepts (vv. 21-23).

X. **In addition to keeping the oneness of the Body, we need to maintain a good order in the Body (1 Cor. 12:18; 2 Cor. 10:13):**

A. God has made definite arrangements and instituted order in the Body (1 Cor. 12:28):

1. We have to know the order of the Body, which is God's assigned pattern in the Body.

2. Every member must be in order and walk in an orderly way (11:34b; 14:33, 40; Col. 2:5).

B. Order in the Body is essential to growth and ministry; lawlessness makes the development of the Body impossible (Eph. 4:16; 1 John 3:4).

C. We must be limited by our measure; when we go beyond our measure, we interfere with the order of the Body (2 Cor. 10:13).

D. We need to maintain a good order in the Body by being subject to one another; then we will keep the one accord (Eph. 5:21; Acts 1:14; 2:46; Rom. 15:6).

Day 6 XI. **There should be only one work in the Lord's recovery—the work of the one Body (Eph. 4:12; 1 Cor. 15:58; 16:10):**

A. We must all see the Body and do the work of the Body (Eph. 1:22-23; 4:12).

B. All the co-workers should do the same one work universally for the Body of Christ (Rom. 12:4-5; 1 Cor. 12:12-13, 24-27; Eph. 4:12).

C. The regions of the work should not divide the churches (Gal. 2:7-8).

D. "Whenever God's children see the oneness of the Body, they will also see the oneness of the work, and they will be delivered out of individualistic work into the work of the Body" (*The Collected Works of Watchman Nee,* vol. 37, p. 244).

XII. In order to keep the oneness of the universal Body of Christ, we need to be blended together (1 Cor. 12:24):

A. The word *blended* means to be adjusted, harmonized, tempered, and mingled, implying the losing of distinctions.

B. Blending requires us to be crossed out and to be by the Spirit to dispense Christ for the sake of the Body (Matt. 16:24; Rom. 8:4; Gal. 5:16, 24-25; Eph. 3:8; 4:12, 16).

C. We should have the blending of all the members of the Body, the blending of all the churches in certain districts, the blending of all the co-workers, and the blending of all the elders.

D. This blending is for the building up of the universal Body of Christ to consummate the New Jerusalem as the final goal of God's economy according to His good pleasure (1:9-10, 23; 3:8-10; Rev. 21:2).

Morning Nourishment

Eph. Being diligent to keep the oneness of the Spirit in the
4:3-4 uniting bond of peace: one Body and one Spirit, even
as also you were called in one hope of your calling.
1 Cor. For even as the body is one and has many members,
12:12-13 yet all the members of the body, being many, are one
body, so also is the Christ. For also in one Spirit we
were all baptized into one Body...

The Lord's recovery is mainly to bring us back to the genuine oneness, to the unique Husband, to the one Body, and to the one Spirit. If we lose this oneness, we are no longer in the Lord's recovery. Rather, we are repeating the history of Christianity, which is a history of divisions.

Many Christians do not care about this matter of division. They say, "The Lord is not narrow. God is omnipresent. Why are you so narrow?" If we know the Bible, we shall see that with respect to division God is more than narrow....Read Deuteronomy 12, 14, 15, and 16 and see how narrow our God is. He told His people that they had no right to worship Him in the place of their choosing. Rather, they had to go to the unique place which He had designated for the worship of God. (*The Spirit and the Body,* p. 181)

Today's Reading

The recovery is based upon the truth that Christ has only one Body....To keep the oneness of the Body is actually to keep the oneness of the Spirit because the Spirit is the reality and the essence of the Body. Paul says in Ephesians 4:3 that we should keep the oneness of the Spirit in the uniting bond of peace. (*Further Consideration of the Eldership, the Region of Work, and the Care for the Body of Christ,* pp. 28, 30)

In the Lord's recovery, we have one name and one Spirit. We all meet in the name of Jesus Christ, and we all meet in the mingled spirit—in the regenerated human spirit indwelt by the Holy Spirit. We gather together in this spirit, not in our concept, desire, preference, or choice. Furthermore, in our meeting we should not leave the cross, which is typified by the altar in front of the tabernacle.

At the entrance of the church there is the cross, and in order to meet as the church we must experience the cross. The flesh, the self, and the natural man cannot be in the church; they must be crucified. Therefore, we meet in the name of the Lord Jesus, in the mingled spirit, and with the cross. This is the place where we meet, and here we have the oneness which we endeavor to keep in the unique name of the Lord. (*Life-study of Deuteronomy,* p. 80)

Every truth in the Bible has two sides....The church has two aspects: the universal aspect and the local aspect. Universally, the church is uniquely one. Locally, however, the church is expressed in many localities. Therefore, the one universal church becomes the many local churches. God is expressed in Christ, Christ is expressed in the church, and the church is expressed in the local churches.

All the local churches are the one unique Body of Christ in the universe (Eph. 4:4)....This one universal church, the one Body, comprises all the local churches.

The local churches are the local expressions of the Body of Christ (1 Cor. 12:27; Eph. 2:22). There is only one Body, but there are many expressions. Universally, all the churches are one Body, and locally, every local church is a local expression of that universal Body. Therefore, a local church is not the Body but only a part of the Body, an expression of the Body.

In Matthew 16:18 the Lord said, "I will build My church." Here the church...must be the universal church. But in Acts and the Epistles there are many references to "the churches"—the churches in Syria, the churches in Asia, the churches in Macedonia, the churches in Galatia. The Bible first refers to one church and then to many churches because the one church, the universal church, is the totality of all the churches, and all the churches are local constituents of the one universal church, the unique Body of Christ. (*The Conclusion of the New Testament,* pp. 2149, 2156)

Further Reading: The Spirit and the Body, ch. 18; *Five Emphases in the Lord's Recovery,* chs. 1, 4; *The Conclusion of the New Testament,* msg. 200

Enlightenment and inspiration: _____

_____

_____

_____

Morning Nourishment

John   That they all may be one; even as You, Father, are
17:21-22 in Me and I in You, that they also may be in Us; that
          the world may believe that You have sent Me. And
          the glory which You have given Me I have given to
          them, that they may be one, even as We are one.

According to the divine revelation of the New Testament, the
church ground is constituted of three crucial elements….The first
element…is the unique oneness of the universal Body of Christ,
which is called "the oneness of the Spirit" (Eph. 4:3). This is the oneness that the Lord prayed for in John 17. It is a oneness of the mingling of the processed Triune God with all the believers in Christ.
This oneness is in the name of the Father (John 17:6, 11), denoting
the Father's person, in which is the Father's life. This oneness is
even in the Triune God through sanctification by His holy word as
the truth (John 17:14-21). This oneness is ultimately in the divine
glory for the expression of the Triune God (John 17:22-24). Such a
oneness was imparted into the spirit of all the believers in Christ
in their regeneration by the Spirit of life with Christ as the divine
life; this oneness has become the basic element of the church
ground. (*A Brief Presentation of the Lord's Recovery*, p. 28)

Today's Reading

The second element of the church ground is the unique ground
of the locality in which a local church is established and exists.
The New Testament presents us a clear picture that all the local
churches, as the expression of the universal church—the universal
Body of Christ—are located in their respective cities….Every city
as the boundary in which a church exists is the local ground of that
church. Such a unique ground of locality preserves the church from
being divided by many different matters as different grounds.

The third element of the church ground is the reality of the
Spirit of oneness, expressing the unique oneness of the universal
Body of Christ on the unique ground of locality of a local church.
…[This element] is the reality of the Spirit, who is the living real-
ity of the divine Trinity (1 John 5:6; John 16:13). It is by this Spirit

that the oneness of the Body of Christ becomes real and living. It is also through this Spirit that the ground of locality is applied in life and not in legality. And it is by this Spirit that the genuine ground of the church is linked with the Triune God (Eph. 4:3-6). (*A Brief Presentation of the Lord's Recovery,* pp. 28-29)

The ground of oneness is simply the processed Triune God applied to our being....We are not in a oneness produced by adding together those who believe in Christ. In that kind of oneness it is just as easy to have subtraction as it is to have addition. However, once we have been brought into the oneness produced by the application of the processed Triune God to our being, it is very difficult to have any subtraction....The oneness in the churches in the Lord's recovery involves the application of the Triune God to our inward being.

The oneness revealed in the Bible is the mingling of the processed Triune God with His chosen people....[It] is a mingling of persons, a mingling of the divine person, the Triune God, with human persons who believe in Christ. The Triune God who is mingled with us has passed through the process of incarnation, human living, crucifixion, and resurrection. That genuine oneness referring to such a marvelous mingling is the clear revelation in John 17 and Ephesians 4. (*The Genuine Ground of Oneness,* pp. 81-82, 86)

In Revelation the golden lampstand signifies the church as the embodiment of the Triune God....That the church is the embodiment of the Triune God corresponds with Ephesians 4. Ephesians 4:4-6 speaks of one Body and one Spirit, one Lord, and one God and Father of all, who is over all and through all and in all. This indicates that the church is the mingling of the Triune God with the Body. This corresponds with the golden lampstands in Revelation. The church is the Triune God completely mingled with His redeemed people as one to become a golden lampstand shining locally to express God Himself. (*The Four Crucial Elements of the Bible—Christ, the Spirit, Life, and the Church,* p. 141)

Further Reading: A Brief Presentation of the Lord's Recovery, secs. VI-VIII; *The Genuine Ground of Oneness,* chs. 5-7

Enlightenment and inspiration: _____

_____

_____

_____

Morning Nourishment

John ...Jesus spoke to them, saying, I am the light of the
8:12 world; he who follows Me shall by no means walk in
darkness, but shall have the light of life.

Rev. And the city has no need of the sun or of the moon
21:23 that they should shine in it, for the glory of God illu-
mined it, and its lamp is the Lamb.

22:1 And he showed me a river of water of life...

John ...Holy Father, keep them in Your name, which You
17:11 have given to Me, that they may be one even as We are.

1 Cor. The churches of Asia greet you....
16:19

God Himself is one. Oneness is His nature. In all God's acts
we see one origin, one element, and one essence. In God's creation we see one God and one corporate man. In His selection
we also have the one God and one man. Moreover, in the church we
have the one Spirit and one new man. Eventually, in the New
Jerusalem we have the unique Triune God in the one city charac-
terized by the one throne, the one street, the one river, and the
one tree. Therefore, the oneness about which we are speaking is
not a partial oneness; it is a great, complete, comprehensive oneness, a oneness in entirety....If we see the vision of the oneness of
entirety,...we shall be delivered from every kind of division.

What is the essence of this great oneness, the oneness in
entirety? The essence of this oneness is life and light. (*The Genuine Ground of Oneness,* pp. 19-20)

Today's Reading

The Triune God with His glory keeps the oneness of the believers. We are not kept in oneness by teachings or doctrines. We are
preserved in oneness by life and light. The Triune God Himself is
the life, and His word with His speaking is the light. By this life
and this light the oneness is maintained. This is the reason Ephesians 4 relates the oneness of the church, the Body of Christ, to
the Triune God, to the Spirit, the Lord, and God the Father.

Firstly, we are enlightened through the Lord's speaking. Then
we receive the supply of life. Eventually, however, the life brings in

more light....Light, life, and oneness go together. The more light, the more life; the more life, the more oneness; and the more oneness, the more light. This cycle of light, life, and oneness preserves the oneness....Through this abundant supply of life the oneness of the New Jerusalem will be forever maintained. It will not be possible for there to be any division. The light will shine throughout the city, and the life will water and supply the city. This life and light will eliminate the possibility of division. Even the nations that surround the new city will be one. At that time, all things in heaven and on earth will be headed up in Christ (Eph. 1:10). This will be the ultimate, universal, and eternal oneness.... This oneness will be kept and preserved in life and with light. (*The Genuine Ground of Oneness,* pp. 26-28)

Perhaps there is a group that has no special name, teaching, or fellowship and that does not insist upon its own administration. We still need to examine whether or not they are willing to open themselves to have fellowship with all the other local churches on earth. Suppose those in this group say, "...We don't like to have fellowship with the other churches";...then they have become a local sect. They are no longer a local church, for a local church is part of the Body, one among many other local churches. Thus, a genuine local church must be open to the other churches. If they isolate themselves from the other churches, they are a local sect.

Today is a day of division and confusion, and we should not accept any group blindly. Rather, we must check whether or not they have a special name, a special teaching, or a special practice. We need to see whether or not they insist upon their own administration, and we must inquire if they are open to all the local churches throughout the world. If they pass all these tests, then they are a genuine local church. But if they cannot pass them, we must hesitate as far as recognizing them as a church is concerned. (*The Spirit and the Body,* pp. 213-214)

Further Reading: The Genuine Ground of Oneness, chs. 1-3; *The Spirit and the Body,* ch. 20; *Young People's Training,* ch. 14*

Enlightenment and inspiration: _____

_____

_____

_____

Morning Nourishment

1 Cor.
1:10
Now I beseech you, brothers, through the name of our Lord Jesus Christ, that you all speak the same thing and *that* there be no divisions among you, but *that* you be attuned in the same mind and in the same opinion.

Col.
1:18
And He is the Head of the Body, the church; He is the beginning, the Firstborn from the dead, that He Himself might have the first place in all things.

John
17:14, 17
I have given them Your word... Sanctify them in the truth; Your word is truth.

Although the children of Israel destroyed the places wherein the nations served their gods upon the mountains and hills and under the green trees, and although the temple was built in Jerusalem, eventually the very things that had been destroyed came back.

To set up a high place is to have a division. Hence, the significance of high places is division. God's intention with the children of Israel in the Old Testament was that His people be kept in oneness in order to worship Him in a proper way. To preserve the oneness of His people, God required that they come to the unique place of His choice. The high places, however, were a substitute and an alternative for this unique place....The unique place, Jerusalem, signifies oneness, whereas the high places signify division. Just as all manner of evil and abominable things were related to the setting up of the high places, so, in New Testament terms, all manner of evil is related to division. (*The Genuine Ground of Oneness,* pp. 97-98)

Today's Reading

Jeroboam made two calves of gold, putting one in Bethel and the other in Dan, in order to distract his people from worshipping God in Jerusalem (1 Kings 12:25-30). God had ordained that His people come together three times a year in Jerusalem. Jeroboam was afraid that the ten tribes would return to their rightful king if they went to worship God in Jerusalem. Thus, he set up two worship centers, saying that it was not convenient to travel to Jerusalem. The excuse of convenience also is used to justify today's denominations. Jeroboam's apostasy broke God's ordination of having one unique worship center in the holy land for keeping the unity, the one-ness, of the children of Israel (Deut. 12:2-18). This became a great sin and caused the people to worship idols. (*Life-study of 1 & 2 Kings*, p. 54)

Sanctification through the word of truth results in oneness. The sanctifying word, the sanctifying Spirit, the sanctifying life, and the sanctifying God are all one. Therefore, if we are being sanctified, we can be nothing else but one. We are one spontaneously because all the factors of division are taken away.

The first of these factors is worldliness. As long as you love the world in a certain aspect, that aspect of worldliness becomes a cause of division. It separates you from the brothers and sisters. Anyone who is worldly is through with oneness.

Another cause of division is ambition....Ambition undermines from within. We all must admit that we are ambitious. What can kill our ambition?...I can testify from experience...that when we con-tact the Lord through the Word and allow Him to infuse Himself into us, the truth thus imparted into our being kills our ambition.

A third cause of division is self-exaltation, which usually accompanies ambition....Self-exaltation...causes division among the saints. Therefore, in order to keep the genuine oneness, we must learn not to exalt ourselves.

The fourth factor of division is opinion and concept....We should not hold to our own opinion but simply pursue the Lord's goal: the recovery of Christ as life and as everything for the build-ing up of the church. Those who have been with me throughout the years can testify that I do not insist on anything except Christ as life and as everything to us for the church.

The four factors of division—worldliness, ambition, self-exaltation, and opinion—can be dealt with only by the sanctify-ing truth....[As you] contact the Lord every morning, touch the living Word, and have the divine reality infused into your being,... the factors of division are overcome. (*Truth Messages*, pp. 49-52)

Further Reading: The Genuine Ground of Oneness, ch. 8; *Life-study of 1 & 2 Kings*, msg. 8; *Truth Messages*, ch. 5

Enlightenment and inspiration: _____

_____

_____

_____

Morning Nourishment

John 17:23 I in them, and You in Me, that they may be perfected into one, that the world may know that You have sent Me and have loved them even as You have loved Me.

1 Cor. 12:18 But now God has placed the members, each one of them, in the body, even as He willed.

2 Cor. 10:13 ...We will not boast beyond *our* measure but according to the measure of the rule which the God of measure has apportioned to us, to reach even as far as you.

In order to be one, we need to be saved from worldliness, ambition, self-exaltation, and concepts. No matter how gentle or meek we may be, in ourselves we are still ambitious. But when we move out of ourselves and into the Triune God, into the "Us" (John 17:21), our ambition is swallowed up. In the Triune God there is no room for ambition. In the universe there is just one place where there is no ambition, and that place is the Triune God. To the Triune God, ambition is a foreign element....I can testify that the only way to be free from ambition is to move out of ourselves and into the Triune God.

In the Triune God there is no ambition, in the glory of the Father there is no self-exaltation, and in the place where Christ lives and reigns there are no opinions and concepts. In this realm ambition is swallowed up, self-exaltation disappears, and concepts and opinions are killed. Here there is no evil; instead, there is the genuine oneness....The genuine oneness is versus evil. We need a oneness that is so genuine, real, and pure. (*Truth Messages*, pp. 68-69, 71)

Today's Reading

The ministry of the Body is not determined by natural things. A member functions in the Body according to what he has received from the Lord. It is according to the "measure of faith" (Rom. 12:3, 6). At the same time, it is according to God's assigned order. Therefore, we have to seek revelation and experience from Christ so that we can have something to supply the Body, and we have to know the order of the Body, which is God's assigned pattern in the Body. We must be willing to be limited to our measure. As soon as we go beyond it, we go beyond the authority of the Head and move out from under the anointing.

When we go beyond our measure, we interfere with the order of the Body. The Body of Christ is an organic life; it operates without any human arrangement. All the members must receive life from the Head and function in proper order. If our relationship with the Head is proper, we will keep our place in the Body spontaneously.

The life of the Body necessitates drastic dealings with the natural life. We must be broken before we will submit to the representative authority in the Body and be willing to minister and be ministered unto in our sovereignly ordained place. God cannot allow lawlessness to come into His church, because this makes the development of the Body impossible. He cannot allow any human head to raise itself, because this also hinders the development of the Body and denies the headship of Christ. Any desire on the part of a believer to exercise authority is contrary to the life of the Body. Christ alone is the Head, and we are all members one of another. If anyone claims to have a revelation of the Body yet is not in subjection to the authority of the Body or properly related to the other members, the claim is false. As soon as we truly see the Body, we will also see the need of obedience and mutual relatedness. Submission is one outstanding characteristic of those who are familiar with the life of the Body.

God has made definite arrangements and instituted order in the Body of Christ. We must be careful to discern the Body, as 1 Corinthians 11:29 charges us to do. We cannot be careless in the Body and make proposals lightly or overstep presumptuously. Every member must be in proper order and walk in an orderly way. Authority is ordained by the Lord; no one can be an authority in himself, and no one can elect others to be an authority. Authority comes from the Lord's arrangement and is for the Body life. We should be clear about our position in the Body and maintain our position. In the Body life, we all must walk according to the order in the Body. (Watchman Nee, *The Mystery of Christ,* pp. 44-45, 48-49)

Further Reading: Truth Messages, chs. 6-7; *The Mystery of Christ,* ch. 8; *Further Consideration of the Eldership, the Region of Work, and the Care for the Body of Christ,* ch. 2

Enlightenment and inspiration: _____

_____

_____

_____

Morning Nourishment

Eph. **For the perfecting of the saints unto the work of the**
4:12 **ministry, unto the building up of the Body of Christ.**
1 Cor. **...If Timothy comes, see that he is with you without fear;**
16:10 **for he is working the work of the Lord, even as I am.**
12:24 **...But God has blended the body together...**

The regions of the work should not divide the churches. There were regions in Paul's time, the Jewish and the Gentile, but they never divided the churches.

At the time of the early apostles, the churches were all one in the Spirit and in practice, but it is not so much like this today among us....All the co-workers in all the regions should do the same one work universally for the unique Body. We should do only one work. There should not be several works in the Lord's recovery. In the past there were several works in the recovery. This is still lingering among us. There is the risk and the danger that these different works will issue in divisions. We have to consider our present situation so that we can eliminate the number of works. The work should be just one. Even Paul and Peter did not carry out two works. Even though they worked in different regions, they had only one work to build up the Body of Christ. (*Further Consideration of the Eldership, the Region of Work, and the Care for the Body of Christ*, pp. 18, 20-21)

Today's Reading

I hope that we will consider our present situation before the Lord. Are we doing the same one work for the recovery? If not, we should let the Lord have the freedom to adjust us. Thank the Lord that due to the riches of the truth, the Lord's recovery is being welcomed everywhere on the earth. In the Lord's move in His recovery, there should only be one work, not different works. Our situation is different from this. We have different works without any consciousness. This is dangerous.

In Paul's time, because of the lack of modern transportation and communication, it would have been logical to have the work divided. However, there was only one work. Today the globe has been made small by modern conveniences....Despite this we do not have one work but many works. If we stay in this situation, a negative result may come out eventually. We do have an existing problem among us. I hope that we would reconsider our situation. (*Further Consideration of the Eldership, the Region of Work, and the Care for the Body of Christ,* p. 21)

God has blended the Body together (1 Cor. 12:24). The word *blended* also means adjusted, harmonized, tempered, and mingled. God has blended the Body, adjusted the Body, harmonized the Body, tempered the Body, and mingled the Body. The Greek word for *blended* implies the losing of distinctions.

In order to be harmonized, blended, adjusted, mingled, and tempered in the Body life, we have to go through the cross and be by the Spirit, dispensing Christ to others for the sake of the Body of Christ. The co-workers and elders must learn to be crossed out. Whatever we do should be by the Spirit to dispense Christ. Also, what we do should not be for our interest and according to our taste but for the church. As long as we practice these points, we will have the blending.

All of these points mean that we should fellowship. When a co-worker does anything, he should fellowship with the other co-workers. An elder should fellowship with the other elders. Fellowship tempers us; fellowship adjusts us; fellowship harmonizes us; and fellowship mingles us....Fellowship requires us to stop when we are about to do something. In our coordination in the church life, in the Lord's work, we all have to learn not to do anything without fellowship.

Among us we should have the blending of all the individual members of the Body of Christ, the blending of all the churches in certain districts, the blending of all the co-workers, and the blending of all the elders. Blending means that we should always stop to fellowship with others. Then we will receive many benefits. If we isolate and seclude ourselves, we will lose much spiritual profit. Learn to fellowship. Learn to be blended. (*The Divine and Mystical Realm,* pp. 86-87)

Further Reading: Further Consideration of the Eldership, the Region of Work, and the Care for the Body of Christ, ch. 1; The Divine and Mystical Realm, ch. 6; The Practical Points concerning Blending, chs. 1-3

Enlightenment and inspiration: _____

_____

_____

_____

Hymns, #831

1   The unity of Church is but
      The saints in oneness living;
   The Spirit which indwelleth them
      This oneness ever giving.
   Thus it is realized and called
      The unity of Spirit;
   'Tis based upon the common faith
      Which all the saints inherit.

2   This precious faith of all the saints,
      Is constituted solely
   Of Christ and His redemptive work,
      Which are unique and holy.
   In this the saints are truly one,
      Together all agreeing,
   And it is from this common faith
      The Church came into being.

3   The Church within the universe
      Is one as Christ's possession;
   The Church must therefore locally
      Be one in her expression;
   For all her elements are one—
      One God, one Lord, one Spirit,
   One faith, baptism, Body too,
      One hope all saints inherit.

4   This oneness is the Church's ground,
      The ground of common standing,
   The only ground of unity
      The Spirit is demanding.
   The Church in actual practise thus
      May keep her vital union,
   And her expressions locally
      Be built up in communion.

5   Lord, help us ever strive to keep
      This unity by taking
   The Church's ground of unity,
      The Body-life partaking,
   That all Thy heart's profound desire
      May fully be effected,
   And God's eternal purpose may
      Completely be perfected.

Composition for prophecy with main point and sub-points:

Albert + Jenny
Paul + Irene - Joshua

The Lord's Recovery of Prophesying as the Excelling Gift for the Building Up of the Church as the Body of Christ

Scripture Reading: 1 Cor. 14:1, 3-5, 12, 24-26, 31-32, 39; Eph. 4:11-16

Day 1   **I. Prophesying is the excelling gift for the building up of the church as the Body of Christ; to prophesy in 1 Corinthians 14 is not in the sense of predicting, foretelling, but in the sense of speaking for the Lord and speaking forth the Lord to dispense Christ into people (vv. 1, 3-5, 12, 24-26, 31-32).**

II. Moses desired that all of God's people would be prophets for prophesying; the apostle Paul taught that we all can prophesy, and he charged us to pursue, to desire earnestly, and to seek to prophesy (Num. 11:29; 1 Cor. 14:1, 12, 31, 39; cf. 1 Thes. 5:20).

III. To prohibit prophesying is a sin before God (Amos 2:12b; 7:12-13, 16-17; Jer. 11:21-23).

Day 2   **IV. Among the three functions of the prophet, the priest, and the king, the function of the prophet is the highest, because the prophets can receive and secure the word of God directly:**

A. In the Old Testament the prophets could reprove, instruct, and teach the kings (2 Sam. 12:1-14), and they could also teach the priests (Hag. 2:10-19; Mal. 1:6—2:9); in the New Testament all the believers are regenerated to be priests and kings (1 Pet. 2:5, 9; Rev. 1:6), but to be a prophet depends upon our seeking, our desiring earnestly (1 Cor. 14:1, 12, 39).

B. All the believers have the capacity and the obligation to prophesy (vv. 31, 24); the Spirit is always ready to speak and expects to speak

with us and through us, so we must cooperate with the speaking Spirit of God by standing
against our natural man with its disposition
and habit (2 Sam. 23:2; Acts 6:10; 2 Tim. 4:2).

  C. Prophesying makes us overcomers; prophesying is the function of the overcomers (Rev. 1:20;
2:1, 7).

V. **According to the New Testament there are
three kinds of prophets:**

  A. The prophets in Ephesians 4:11-12 are those
particularly ordained by God for the perfecting
of the saints (cf. 1 Cor. 12:29).

  B. The prophets in Acts 21:8-9 are those who can
predict for God.

  C. The prophets in 1 Corinthians 14 are those who
speak for God and speak forth God in the meetings of the church for the church's building
up; all the believers can be this kind of prophet
(vv. 1, 5, 31).

Day 3 VI. **The proper church meeting for the building
up of the church described in 1 Corinthians
14:26 is a meeting of mutuality in which
"each one has," a meeting in which we "can
all prophesy one by one" (v. 31), a meeting
in which "he who prophesies builds up the
church" (v. 4); the fulfillment of this word
in the Lord's present recovery is eternally
significant.**

VII. **First Corinthians 14:26 as a part of the holy
Word needs to be fulfilled for the Body of
Christ to be built up; without this organic
building, the Lord's prophecy in Matthew
16:18 cannot be fulfilled, and the church as
the bride cannot be made ready for Christ as
the Bridegroom.**

Day 4 VIII. **To meet according to 1 Corinthians 14:26, we
must desire and learn to prophesy and live a
prophesying life by being revived every
morning and by living an overcoming life**

every day (vv. 1, 12, 31; Prov. 4:18; Lam. 3:22-24; Psa. 119:147-148; Rev. 2:7; 21:7; 1 John 1:6-7).

Day 5 IX. **We must live a prophesying life with the following qualifications:**

A. We must "bring out the precious from the worthless" (Jer. 15:19).

B. We must love the Lord, be close to Him, and be one with Him (1:8-9; Psa. 73:28a; 1 Cor. 2:9, 15; cf. 14:31-32).

C. We must have an intimacy with God; our relationship with God must be personal, affectionate, private, and spiritual (Psa. 25:14; S. S. 1:1-4).

D. We must be those who bring every problem into the presence of God, contacting God to receive the word from God (Psa. 73:3, 17).

E. We must pray for the ministry of the word (Acts 6:4).

F. We must be ones who are always rejoicing, unceasingly praying, giving thanks in everything, not quenching the Spirit, and not despising prophecies (1 Thes. 5:16-20).

G. We must let the word of Christ dwell in us richly in all wisdom, teaching and admonishing one another with psalms and hymns and spiritual songs, singing with grace in our hearts to God (Col. 3:16).

H. We must be filled with the knowledge of God's word to acquire an adequate divine vocabulary (Luke 1:46-55; Acts 5:20; 1 Pet. 4:11).

I. We must be filled with the consummated Spirit essentially and economically (Matt. 5:12; Acts 13:52; 4:8, 31; 13:9; 2:38; 5:32b).

Day 6 X. **We must see the composition of a proper prophecy according to the way of 1 Corinthians 14:**

A. The composition of a prophecy comprises the knowledge and experience of God, Christ, and spiritual things and the utterance to speak these forth.

B. The composition of a prophecy comprises the sight under the divine enlightenment concerning the situation and environment in which we are.

C. The composition of a prophecy comprises the instant inspiration of the Spirit that stirs up our spirit to speak (Acts 5:20).

D. In speaking forth a proper prophecy, we should not adhere to personal experiences, testimonies, feelings, thoughts, opinions, affections, and reactions to any persons, matters, and things (2 Cor. 4:5).

XI. **The direct building up of the organic Body of Christ is by the Body itself, that is, by all the members of Christ each functioning in his own measure, mainly in prophesying— speaking for the Lord (Eph. 4:16; 1 Cor. 14:4b, 12, 31; Heb. 10:25).**

XII. **Those of us who have seen this vision will be burdened to sacrifice ourselves as martyrs so that the Lord can have a way to fulfill Ephesians 4:11-16 for the purpose of having the building up of His organic Body through each saint being perfected to prophesy, to speak Christ, so that there will be meetings all over the earth that are full of mutuality according to 1 Corinthians 14:26.**

Morning Nourishment

Moses

Num. ...Oh that all Jehovah's people were prophets, that
11:29 Jehovah would put His Spirit upon them!

Paul

1 Cor. For you can all prophesy one by one that all may
14:31 learn and all may be encouraged.

We have to consider what it means to prophesy. According to
our natural concept, to prophesy is to merely predict, or foretell.
This concept is prevailing in the Pentecostal movement. In 1963
some..."prophesied" that there would be a great earthquake in
Los Angeles and that the entire city would fall into the ocean. Of
course, such an event did not take place....The meaning of prophesying has been spoiled by the Pentecostal teaching and practice.
When those in the Pentecostal movement talk about prophesying
according to 1 Corinthians 14, they talk about it in a wrong way.

We must admit that prophesying does convey the thought of
foretelling, predicting. Most people, whether Christians or non-
Christians, understand prophesying in this way. But we all have
to see that prophesying in chapter fourteen of 1 Corinthians is not
used in this sense at all. The interpretation of prophesying as
predicting does not fit in the context of this entire chapter. Prophesying in 1 Corinthians 14 is not in the sense of predicting, foretelling, but in the sense of speaking for the Lord, speaking forth
the Lord, to dispense Christ to people.

Even in the Old Testament, to prophesy is not mainly to predict.
The book of Isaiah the prophet has sixty-six chapters, and most of
these chapters are not predicting but are speaking for the Lord....
Chapter one of Isaiah, in which he rebuked the people of Israel, is
a chapter of his speaking for the Lord. The main denotation of the
word *prophesy* both in Hebrew and in Greek is to speak for the
Lord. When we speak for the Lord, even if we do not foretell, our
speaking is the genuine prophesying. To prophesy is to speak God
into people. (*The Advance of the Lord's Recovery Today,* p. 98)

Today's Reading

Moses desired all of God's people to be prophets for prophesying
(Num. 11:29b),...[and] the apostle Paul taught that we all can

prophesy (1 Cor. 14:31). God desires that each of the believers prophesy, that is, speak for and speak forth Him.

Paul charged us not to despise prophesying (1 Thes. 5:20). Those who have rejected the Lord's ministry, the Lord's speaking, today are despising prophesying. Some opposing ones have said that we can simply read the Bible itself without the help of the Recovery Version or the Life-study messages. However, if you merely read the Bible in that way, you will not receive much. The Bible has been interpreted by the seeking saints for the past twenty centuries, beginning from the so-called church fathers, who spoke concerning the Divine Trinity. Without their interpretation, how could we understand the Trinity today? The words *Trinity* and *triune* are not written in the Bible; but the fact of the Trinity was discovered by the church fathers. They did a marvelous job concerning this matter, and through the centuries their interpretation has come to us. We need the interpreted Word.

The Recovery Version with the Life-study messages can be considered as the crystallization of the understanding of the holy Word, which the seeking saints have interpreted throughout the past twenty centuries. This is the reason that I am burdened to have the life-study of the entire Bible. If we do not understand a certain part of the book of Genesis, we can go to the *Life-study of Genesis* for help...to enter into the divine thought.

To prohibit prophesying is a sin before God (Amos 2:12b; 7:12-13; Jer. 11:21). Amaziah the priest charged Amos to stop speaking, to stop prophesying. Because of this, Amaziah suffered a curse. The Lord said through Amos that the wife of Amaziah would become a harlot and that his children would be killed (Amos 7:16-17). Those who stopped Jeremiah from prophesying also suffered calamity (Jer. 11:21-23). (*The Practice of the Church Life according to the God-ordained Way*, pp. 53-54)

Further Reading: The Practice of the Church Life according to the God-ordained Way, ch. 4; *The Advance of the Lord's Recovery Today*, chs. 6-7

Enlightenment and inspiration: _____

_____

_____

_____

Morning Nourishment

1 Cor. Pursue love, and desire earnestly spiritual *gifts*, but
14:1 especially that you may prophesy.
  3-4 ...He who prophesies speaks building up and encouragement and consolation to men....He who prophesies builds up the church.

To prophesy in function is higher than being a king or a priest. In both the Old and New Testaments, only three kinds of ministries were ordained by God—the ministries of the prophets, the priests, and the kings. In Genesis 20:7 Abraham was called a prophet. At that time among God's people, there were no kings and no official priests....In the Old Testament, God first recognized the function of the prophet, then the function of the priest, and later the function of the king.

In the New Testament, all of the believers are regenerated to be priests and kings (1 Pet. 2:5, 9; Rev. 1:6),...but to be a prophet depends upon our seeking [1 Cor. 14:1]....If you do not desire earnestly and seek to prophesy, you cannot be a prophet. All those who desire to prophesy are like the Nazarites in the Old Testament (Num. 6:1-21), who voluntarily separated themselves unto the Lord.

Among the three functions of the prophet, the priest, and the king, the function of the prophet is the highest. The reason for this is that all three of these functions depend upon God's word. The kings in the Old Testament time could not receive God's word directly. The priests could receive God's word, but not directly. They received God's word indirectly through the breastplate with the Urim and the Thummim (Exo. 28:30). But the prophets, even in the Old Testament time, received God's word directly. For this reason, the prophets could reprove, instruct, and teach the kings (2 Sam. 12:1-14), and they could also teach the priests (Hag. 2:10-19; Mal. 1:6—2:9). Because they can receive and secure the word of God directly, the prophets have the highest function. (*The Practice of the Church Life according to the God-ordained Way*, pp. 54-55)

Today's Reading

According to the New Testament, there are three kinds of

prophets....Ephesians 2:20 says, "Being built upon the foundation of the apostles and prophets." Ephesians 4:11-12 says, "And He Himself gave some as apostles and some as prophets..., for the perfecting of the saints unto the work of the ministry, unto the building up of the Body of Christ." The prophets mentioned in these verses are those particularly ordained by God. The second kind of prophet is one who can predict, like Philip's daughters (Acts 21:8-9). The third kind of prophet is one who speaks for God and speaks forth God in the meetings of the church for the church's building up (1 Cor. 14:3-5).

In speaking of [the] first kind of prophet, Paul said in 1 Corinthians 12:29, "Are all prophets?" Not all of the believers are prophets particularly ordained by God. However, all of the believers can be the third kind of prophet (1 Cor. 14:1, 5, 31). First Corinthians 14:31 says, "You can all prophesy one by one."...This apparent contradiction is solved by the realization that there are different kinds of prophets. (*The Practice of the Church Life according to the God-ordained Way*, pp. 56-57)

Eventually, both the Old and New Testaments end with the overcomers. In the age of typology, the overcomers were the prophets. The prophets took care of God's oracle first. Based upon their oracle, they did exercise, to some extent, God's authority....It was not Nathan who listened to David, but David to Nathan. In this sense, Nathan was God's authority. Thus, all of the genuine prophets were overcomers.

[The overcomers in Revelation 2 and 3] are the fulfillment of the typology of the prophets. Therefore, when the apostle Paul was talking about how the church should meet, he stressed and uplifted prophesying (1 Cor. 14:1, 3-6, 24, 31, 39). Prophesying makes you an overcomer. Speaking Christ into people is prophesying. Prophesying is the function of the overcomers. (*Living a Life according to the High Peak of God's Revelation*, pp. 9-10)

Further Reading: Living a Life according to the High Peak of God's Revelation, chs. 1-2

Enlightenment and inspiration: _____

_____

_____

_____

Morning Nourishment

1 Cor. 14:23-24	If...the whole church comes together,...and all speak in tongues, and some unlearned *in tongues* or unbelievers enter, will they not say that you are insane? But if all prophesy and some unbeliever or unlearned person enters, he is convicted by all, he is examined by all.
26	...Whenever you come together, each one has a psalm, has a teaching, has a revelation, has a tongue, has an interpretation. Let all things be done for building up.

In 1937 [Brother Nee fellowshipped] concerning the need to recover the church meeting of mutuality revealed in 1 Corinthians 14 [see *The Normal Christian Church Life*]....At that time, however, we did not find a way to replace the traditional way of one speaking and the rest listening with this scriptural practice. In 1948 Brother Nee fellowshipped with us again along these lines [see *Church Affairs*]....He told us that the so-called Sunday morning service in which one man speaks and the rest listen is unscriptural and according to the customs of the nations (2 Kings 17:8). He proposed that we put this kind of meeting aside and encourage all the saints to go out and preach the gospel on the Lord's Day. Within a short time,...however, the Communists took over mainland China, so we did not have a chance to work out his burden.

All of us have to pay the price to enter into the scriptural way of meeting revealed in 1 Corinthians 14. We need to practice 1 Corinthians 14:26—"Whenever you come together, each one has." To carry out God's New Testament economy, His eternal plan for the New Testament age, all of us who are His children should learn to exercise the capacities in the divine life He has given us.

Paul says we can all prophesy one by one (1 Cor. 14:31). This indicates that we all have the capacity to prophesy. Paul says in verses 23 and 24 that when "the whole church comes together in one place.... But if all prophesy...." This means we have the obligation to prophesy. (*The Advance of the Lord's Recovery Today*, pp. 172-173, 176)

Today's Reading

In 1984 I realized that the Lord's recovery had nearly come to a standstill. We had become dormant. By the Lord's mercy, He caused us to realize that we needed to get into His recovery in an ultimate way. Many scriptural truths and practices have been recovered by the Lord throughout the history of the church,…but there is at least one thing He has not recovered. He has not yet recovered the way to meet.…He said that the church has to practice 1 Corinthians 14:26. This is a big item in the New Testament that needs to be recovered. Where can we see a meeting in which the Christians come together, and each one has something? In 1 Corinthians 14:26 Paul used the word "has" five times—each one has a psalm, has a teaching, has a revelation, has a tongue, has an interpretation. Brother Nee called this kind of meeting a meeting of mutuality. This is different from the customs of the nations. Whenever the nations have a gathering, only one person speaks and the rest listen. This practice is worldly and natural.

If we are going to fulfill 1 Corinthians 14:26, we must take care of Ephesians 4:11-16. All the gifted persons have to perfect the saints. Then all the saints will do exactly what the gifted persons do, and each one part of the Body will operate. All the Body of Christ causes the growth of the Body through every part operating. The answer to how 1 Corinthians 14:26 can be fulfilled is in Ephesians 4:11-16.…This is a part of the Lord's recovery and a progression of the Lord's recovery.

We have the assurance from the Word that 1 Corinthians 14:26 and Ephesians 4:11-16 must be fulfilled. The main thing that these two portions of the Word reveal to us is the proper church meeting for the building up of the organic Body of Christ, not for the building up of a congregation. This has to be fulfilled, and this fulfillment is a great part of the Lord's recovery. We have to treasure this revelation and receive it as the glad tidings. We are blessed to be in the Lord's recovery at this time. (*The Excelling Gift for the Building Up of the Church*, pp. 74-76)

Further Reading: The Advance of the Lord's Recovery Today, ch. 10;
   The Excelling Gift for the Building Up of the Church, chs. 1, 6

Enlightenment and inspiration: _____

_____
_____
_____

Morning Nourishment

Prov. But the path of the righteous is like the light of dawn, /
4:18 Which shines brighter and brighter until the full day.
Rev. He who overcomes will inherit these things, and I will
21:7 be God to him, and he will be a son to Me.
1 John If we say that we have fellowship with Him and yet
1:6-7 walk in the darkness, we lie and are not practicing the
truth; but if we walk in the light as He is in the light,
we have fellowship with one another, and the blood of
Jesus His Son cleanses us from every sin.

If we are going to prophesy, we need to live a prophesying life.
First, we need to be revived every morning (Prov. 4:18; Lam. 3:22-
24; Psa. 119:147-148)....[According to Proverbs 4:18], the way of
the just is like the dawn that becomes brighter and brighter until
noontime. Every twenty-four hours there is a new start, a dawn, a
rising sun. This is according to the natural law in God's creation.
We have to go along with this natural law. Every morning, we
have to rise early to contact the Lord, to call on Him, and to be
revived by Him. In Lamentations 3:22-24, Jeremiah says that the
Lord's compassions are new every morning. His compassions are
like the fresh dew in the morning. Every morning we must enjoy
this fresh dew to have a new start, a morning revival.

In addition to being revived every morning, we must also
live an overcoming life every day (Rev. 21:7). After the morning
revival, we should not stop contacting the Lord. We can live a victorious life by fellowshipping with the Lord moment by moment
(1 John 1:6). We also need to walk according to spirit (Rom. 8:4b),
not doing anything outside of the Spirit. We should also speak the
word (the Lord) all the time. Paul charged Timothy to preach the
word in season and out of season (2 Tim. 4:2a)....Such a prophesying life qualifies us to prophesy. (*The Excelling Gift for the Building Up of the Church,* pp. 30-31)

Today's Reading

In Taipei we gave the saints some practical fellowship concerning how to prepare to prophesy in the church meetings on the

Lord's Day. Every week they will cover a chapter of a certain book of the Bible and divide this chapter into six portions for six days. In each section for each day, they choose two or three verses for pray-reading, and they enjoy the Lord with these verses for their morning revival. We charged the saints to write down a short reminder of what the Lord inspired them with in their time with Him in the morning. At the end of the week, they will have six notes of what they were inspired with during the week. On Saturday night they use these notes of their inspiration to compose a prophecy to speak for three minutes. Then they practice it in their homes. They are instructed not to be too long or too short. When they go to the church meeting on the Lord's Day, they have something, thus fulfilling the Lord's word in 1 Corinthians 14:26—"each one has." They do not trust merely in instant inspiration, but they come to the meeting prepared with the riches of Christ that they have enjoyed....The saints need to be perfected to enjoy the Lord, to be saturated with the Word, to pray unceasingly, to fellowship with the Lord moment by moment, to walk in the Spirit, and to speak the Lord in the Spirit at all times. Then they need to learn how to compose a prophecy for the church meetings. I hope that we all would try to practice this for our church meetings.

If only fifteen out of fifty saints prophesy in a meeting of the church, that meeting will be in the third heavens. This is what the Lord desires. Regardless of how long a message is or how good it is, it only covers one main item. But when fifteen prophesy, different points will be covered. This prophesying will touch people's problems in a particular way. Such speaking will not only nourish the saints but also build them up. When one person speaks, only what he has experienced of the riches of Christ is released. When fifteen people speak, the riches of Christ come out of fifteen sources and fifteen portions of Christ are ministered. (*The Excelling Gift for the Building Up of the Church*, pp. 31-32)

Further Reading: The Excelling Gift for the Building Up of the Church, ch. 2

Enlightenment and inspiration: _____
_____
_____

Morning Nourishment

Jer. ...If you bring out the precious from the worthless, /
15:19 You will be as My mouth...
Psa. The intimate counsel of Jehovah is to those who fear
25:14 Him...
Acts But we will continue steadfastly in prayer and in the
6:4 ministry of the word.

The first qualification for prophesying is to take the precious things from the vile, or worthless (Jer. 15:19). God said to Jeremiah, "And if you bring out the precious from the worthless, / You will be as My mouth." In order to speak the word of God, we have to separate all the vile, worthless things from the precious things. We have received many precious things. If we do not keep the precious things separate from the vile things, we will lose the position to be the mouthpiece of God.

To love the Lord, to be close to Him, and to be one with Him is another qualification for those who would prophesy (Jer. 1:8-9; Psa. 73:28a). All of the prophets loved the Lord, were very close to the Lord, and were one with the Lord. We must have the same experience; otherwise, we cannot be prophets.

The intimate counsel of Jehovah belongs to those who fear Him, and His covenant He will make known to them (Psa. 25:14). In order to prophesy, we must have an intimacy with God. Furthermore, we should not think that because we are intimate with God, we can be loose. On the contrary, we must also have a fear that matches our intimacy. In this way we are qualified to be God's mouthpiece. (*The Practice of the Church Life according to the God-ordained Way*, pp. 57-58)

Today's Reading

In Psalm 73 the psalmist was bothered at the prosperity of the wicked (v. 3)....He could not understand until he went into the sanctuary of God, that is, until he contacted God. This shows that he did not want to solve any problem apart from God. He went into the presence of God to get his problem solved; then he received the word from God.

Br. Lee judged Himself.

In Acts 6:4 Peter said, "But we will continue steadfastly in prayer and in the ministry of the word." In order to prophesy, we must pray for the ministry of the word. Without prayer, the ministry of the word will not be enlivened and empowered.

Another qualification for prophesying is to be one who is always rejoicing, unceasingly praying, giving thanks in everything, and quenching not the Spirit concerning prophesying (1 Thes. 5:16-20). ...We all, brothers and sisters alike, have quenched the Spirit too often....We are children of a speaking Father, so we all must speak. Many would say that they do not know how to speak. The way to learn how to speak is to speak....The most victorious, overcoming, and successful Christian is a Christian who is a speaking one. The more you speak, the more you overcome. The purpose for us all to meet together is for all of us to speak.

In order to prophesy, we must let the word of Christ dwell in us richly in all wisdom, teaching and admonishing one another with psalms and hymns and spiritual songs, singing with grace in our hearts to God (Col. 3:16).

To prophesy we must be filled with the Spirit. The Ephesian believers in Acts 19:6 were outwardly filled with the Spirit, and they prophesied....To prophesy is to speak for God, to impart the divine revelations to others.

The practice of prophesying includes at least five items: exercising your spirit, speaking with your mouth open, speaking audibly, speaking in the proper speed, and speaking with the purified and accurate word. You need to exercise your spirit in a definite way with an open mouth. To speak audibly is to speak loud enough for the entire congregation to hear. To speak in the proper speed is not to speak too slowly or too rapidly. To speak with the purified and accurate word is to speak without any wasted words, avoiding "sea stories." (*The Practice of the Church Life according to the God-ordained Way,* pp. 58-59)

Further Reading: The Present Advance of the Lord's Recovery, ch. 5; The Practice of the Church Life according to the God-ordained Way, ch. 4

Enlightenment and inspiration: _____

_____

_____

_____

Morning Nourishment

Acts **Go and stand in the temple and speak to the people**
5:20 **all the words of this life.**
2 Cor. **For we do not preach ourselves but Christ Jesus as**
4:5 **Lord, and ourselves as your slaves for Jesus' sake.**

The composition of a prophecy according to the way in 1 Corinthians 14 comprises, first, the knowledge and experience of God, Christ, and the spiritual things....Second, [it] comprises the utterance to speak forth what we know and have experienced of God, Christ, and the spiritual things. First we need the knowledge and experience; then we need the utterance, that is, the word and the expression. We can compose a brief prophecy and then practice speaking it to ourselves at home. We may even speak it to ourselves ten times. After speaking it several times, we will know how to correct and improve it. Through this kind of practice, we will have the proper utterance. (*The Practice of Prophesying*, pp. 13-14)

Today's Reading

The composition of a prophecy also comprises the sight under the divine enlightenment concerning the situation and environment in which we are. Many among us are not clear about the intrinsic contents of the present turmoil in the Lord's recovery, and some prefer not to be clear. Their attitude is that others should be clear about the situation, but that they should take care only of enjoying Christ. Such an attitude is wrong. The church is our home and our family. If there is a turmoil in our home among our family, we cannot say, "I do not want to know about it. I simply want to enjoy." We must have the sight to see the things taking place among us and the situation of all the saints. If we cannot see clearly, we need to pray, "Lord, show me the real situation. Shine over me and enlighten me. Give me the full enlightenment that I may know the intrinsic contents of the present situation." We must know what is happening in the church, not so that we may take sides with one group of saints against another, but so that we may know the real situation.

The knowledge and the experience of God, Christ, and the spiritual things, the utterance to speak forth what we know and have experienced, and a clear view concerning our situation and environment are the basic preparation for our speaking. In addition, we need the instant inspiration of the indwelling Spirit that stirs up our spirit to speak. We are different from the Old Testament prophets. In the Old Testament, the saints did not have the abiding Spirit indwelling them. They had to wait until the Spirit came upon them before they could speak for the Lord (2 Chron. 15:1; Ezek. 11:5). However, the New Testament says, "The Lord be with your spirit" (2 Tim. 4:22)....Therefore, we should not wait for the Spirit to come upon us; rather, we should exercise our spirit. When we exercise our spirit, the Holy Spirit who is indwelling our spirit will be moved by us, and we will have the inspiration. It is not He who moves us, but it is we who move the indwelling Spirit. If we remain clear with the Lord by confessing our failures, we will have a direct, open fellowship with Him. He is in our spirit, and we are in Him. When we come to the meeting, we need only to exercise our spirit and say, "Lord Jesus, I want to speak." Then He will rise up, and we can speak according to our experience with the utterance we have gained and with the enlightenment that we have. If we do this, everyone will have something to speak in the Lord's Day morning meeting.

We need to practice composing a prophecy according to the way in 1 Corinthians 14. To help us in this matter, we have prepared the book *The Holy Word for Morning Revival.* If we use the contents of this book with the knowledge and experience of God, Christ, and the spiritual things, the utterance to speak forth what we know and have experienced, the sight under the divine enlightenment concerning our situation, and the instant inspiration of the indwelling Spirit through the clear and open fellowship with the Lord in the exercise of our spirit, we can easily compose a prophecy and speak it in the church meeting. (*The Practice of Prophesying,* pp. 14-15)

Further Reading: The Practice of Prophesying, chs. 1, 4; *The Way to Practice the Lord's Present Move,* ch. 3; *The Present Advance of the Lord's Recovery,* ch. 6; *Prophesying in the Church Meetings for the Organic Building Up of the Church as the Body of Christ (Outlines),* outline 6

Enlightenment and inspiration: _____
_____
_____

Hymns, #867

1   As members of the Body
     Christ we would manifest,
  Each learning how to function
     His fulness to express;
  We would not be spectators
     But each as members move,
  None bringing death or damage
     But each our profit prove.

2   As in a team we'd never
     Act independently,
  But in coordination,
     Each would dependent be;
  Not acting by our choosing
     But following the flow,
  Distraction never bringing,
     The Spirit's way we'd know.

3   On Christ we here would focus,
     No other center make;
  With Christ in sweet communion
     His riches to partake.
  He is our Head and content,
     His Body we express;
  Whate'er we do while meeting
     Himself must manifest.

4   Built up in love together,
     Not one would criticize;
  To perfect one another,
     We all would exercise.
  Each one from self delivered,
     The natural life forsakes;
  In grace each trained in spirit
     The Body-life partakes.

Composition for prophecy with main point and sub-points: _____

_____

_____

_____

_____

_____

_____

_____

_____

_____

_____

_____

_____

_____

_____

_____

_____

_____

_____

_____

_____

_____

_____

_____

_____

_____

_____

_____

_____

_____

_____

_____

_____

_____

Responding to Christ's Heavenly Intercession by Praying at the Golden Incense Altar

Scripture Reading: Heb. 7:25; Col. 3:1-4; Exo. 30:1-10

Day 1

I. In His heavenly ministry Christ is interceding, ministering, and executing God's administration, and we need to be those who respond to Christ's activities in His heavenly ministry (Heb. 2:17; 4:14; 7:25-26; 8:1-2; Rev. 5:6; Col. 3:1-4; 1:9; 4:12):

A. As the High Priest, He intercedes; as the heavenly Minister, He ministers; and as the Redeemer with the seven eyes of God, He administers the government of God for the accomplishment of God's purpose (Heb. 7:25-26; 8:1-2; Rev. 5:6).

B. Christ's ministry in the heavens requires our response; we need to become on earth the reflection of Christ's heavenly ministry, praying the prayers of the interceding Christ (Col. 3:1-4; Rom. 8:34):

1. Through our prayer, Christ the Head is given a way to carry out His administration through His Body (Col. 1:9-10, 18; 2:19; 3:1-2; 4:12).

2. As the Head is working in heaven by interceding, ministering, and administrating, we, the Body, are working on earth, responding to the heavenly ministry of Christ and reflecting what He is doing (Heb. 2:17; 4:14; 7:26; 8:1-2; Rev. 5:6).

3. We should aspire to be one with the Lord in His heavenly ministry and to have a heart that is one with His heart, and we should long to be one with Him in His priesthood, ministry, and administration (1 Cor. 6:17).

Day 2

II. In order to respond to Christ's heavenly intercession, we need to see a vision of the golden incense altar (Exo. 30:1-10):

A. The incense altar signifies Christ as the Intercessor (Heb. 7:25; Rom. 8:34).

B. The incense altar is a type of Christ, signifying Christ praying (Exo. 30:1-3).

C. The incense altar is the place from which the activities at all the other places in the tabernacle and the outer court are motivated (Heb. 7:25).

D. Christ's interceding life, His prayer life, is the center of the divine administration (Rom. 8:34; Rev. 8:3-4):

1. The prayer life of Christ is the center of God's execution of His government on earth (John 17).

2. The executing of God's administration is motivated by the prayers offered to Him from the incense altar (Rev. 8:3-4).

3. The prayer offered at the incense altar governs the universe.

4. The incense altar may be regarded as the heavenly white house; everything is motivated, executed, and carried out from this divine center.

E. After His resurrection and ascension, the individual Christ has become the corporate Christ; thus, before God today not only is the individual Christ interceding, but the corporate Christ, the Head with the Body, is interceding as well (1 Cor. 12:12; Acts 12:5, 12):

1. Today the intercessor is not merely Christ Himself but is Christ with His Body (Rom. 8:26-27, 34).

2. Christ the Head is interceding in the heavens, and the church the Body is interceding on earth (Heb. 7:25; Acts 12:5, 12).

3. As the members of Christ and parts of the Body Christ, we cooperate with Christ in His ministry of intercession, carrying out His intercession in our prayers of intercession (Rom. 8:26-27, 34; 1 Tim. 2:1).

Day 3

    F. If we have a vision of the incense altar, our prayer life will be revolutionized; we will pray for the executing of God's purpose, for the carrying out of the divine administration, and for the dispensing of God's supplying grace.

  III. **In order to respond to Christ's heavenly intercession, we need to experience the golden incense altar (Exo. 30:1-10; Rom. 8:26-27; 1 Tim. 2:1):**

    A. We should participate in Christ's interceding life (Eph. 6:18-19; Col. 4:3; 1 Thes. 5:25; 2 Thes. 3:1; Heb. 13:18).

    B. The kind of prayer we have depends on the kind of person we are (Luke 9:54-55; 1 Tim. 2:8; Eph. 6:18; Col. 1:9-10).

Day 4

    C. If we would intercede with Christ at the incense altar, we need to see three crucial matters:

      1. When we pray, we should be in the tabernacle; that is, we should be in God (John 1:14; 14:2-3, 20, 13-14; 15:4a, 7; 17:24, 26b).

      2. When we are about to pray, we should first be satisfied by eating holy food; that is, we should pray with God within us as our energizing supply (1:29; 6:53-56).

      3. When we pray, we should offer incense to God; that is, we should pray with Christ as the incense (Exo. 30:34-38; Rev. 8:3-4).

Day 5

    D. When we pray at the incense altar, there should be neither strange fire nor strange incense in our prayer (Lev. 10:1; Exo. 30:9a):

      1. To have strange fire in our prayer is to have some kind of motive that is natural and that has not been dealt with by the cross (Lev. 10:1).

      2. To have strange incense in our prayer is to have prayer that is not related to Christ (Exo. 30:9a).

Day 6

    E. If we would pray in the tabernacle at the incense altar, we need to be burned to ashes, reduced to nothing (Lev. 6:13; Psa. 20:3; Gal. 2:20; 1 Cor. 1:28b):

1. To be in the tabernacle is to be in God, and the requirement for being in God is that we become nothing (John 15:4a, 5b).

2. If we are burned to ashes, we will no longer be natural (1 Cor. 2:14-15):

   a. Our conduct, our sight, and our virtue equal our natural being, which is versus Christ as God's testimony.

   b. If we would pray at the incense altar, we must no longer have our natural conduct, our natural sight, and our natural virtue.

   c. If we would pray at the incense altar, we must have Christ as our life supply for proper conduct, as our light for proper sight, and as our virtue for us to have a sweet fragrance ascending to God.

F. When we pray at the incense altar, it is difficult for us to be occupied with ourselves; instead, we pray for God's economy, for God's dispensing, for God's move, and for God's recovery (Eph. 1:17-23; 3:14-21; Col. 1:9-10; 4:12).

Morning Nourishment

Heb. 8:1-2 ...We have such a High Priest, who sat down on the right hand of the throne of the Majesty in the heavens, a Minister of the holy places, even of the true tabernacle, which the Lord pitched, not man.

Col. 3:1 If therefore you were raised together with Christ, seek the things which are above, where Christ is, sitting at the right hand of God.

1:9 Therefore we also, since the day we heard of *it*, do not cease praying and asking on your behalf that you may be filled with the full knowledge of His will in all spiritual wisdom and understanding.

To seek the things above and to set our mind on them is to live Christ, to have one living with Him. When Christ prays in heaven, we should pray on earth. This means that there is a transmission between the Christ praying in heaven and us praying on earth. By means of this transmission we may pray in oneness with Him. We respond on earth to Christ's praying in heaven. None of us should be unemployed. We all have the responsibility to respond to Christ's heavenly transmission. We need to live together with Christ by seeking the things which are above and setting our mind on them. Christ is in heaven interceding, ministering, and administrating, and we are on earth responding to Christ's activity in heaven. (*Life-study of Colossians*, p. 532)

Today's Reading

If we seek the things above and have one living with Christ, we shall be wholly occupied with the enterprise of our Master. Our heart will be with Him in heaven, where He is interceding for the churches, supplying the saints, and administrating God's government. This will be our concern, our desire. If we take Christ as life and seek the things which are above in such a way, the lustful members will be put to death, the evil elements in the fallen soul will be put away, and the old man will be put off. Furthermore, we shall automatically put on the new man.

We need to be those who respond to Christ's heavenly ministry.

For centuries, Christ has tried without adequate success to get a people to respond to His ministry in the heavens....Let us be those who tell the Lord that we are one with Him in this ministry.

We need to be impressed with the fact that the Christ who is in heaven is very busy. Consider how many local churches He takes care of throughout the world. Christ's ministry in heaven is all for the goal of building up the Body and forming His bride. However, Christ's ministry in heaven requires our response. We need to become on earth the very reflection of that heavenly ministry. When we seek the things above, we respond to the Lord's heavenly ministry and reflect it. Our experience testifies of this. If in our prayer we are willing to forget insignificant matters and care for the things above, we shall become conscious of the traffic between us and Christ in heaven. We shall sense a current flowing back and forth between Him and us. By means of this kind of prayer, the divine riches are transfused into us. This enables us to be one with others and to be right with everyone. This also issues in the renewing of the new man. Through the heavenly transmission and transfusion, the new man comes into existence in a practical way. Hence, the new man is not produced by teaching; the new man is produced by the heavenly traffic, transaction, and transfusion.

The things above do not include any religion, philosophy, or culture. Instead, they include Christ's priesthood, ministry, and administration with all His activities. It is crucial for us to realize that Christ is our Head and that we are the members of His Body. Christ and we together form a universal man. As the One in heaven, He is the Head, and as those on earth, we are the Body. As the Head is working in heaven by interceding, ministering, and administrating, we, the Body, are working on earth responding to the heavenly ministry of Christ and reflecting what He is doing in heaven. What a tremendous matter this is! (*Life-study of Colossians,* pp. 534, 546-548, 552)

Further Reading: Life-study of Colossians, msgs. 60-62

Enlightenment and inspiration: _____

_____

_____

_____

Morning Nourishment

Exo. **And you shall make an altar on which to burn**
30:1 **incense...**

Heb. **Hence also He is able to save to the uttermost those**
7:25 **who come forward to God through Him, since He**
lives always to intercede for them.

Rev. **And another Angel came and stood at the altar, hav-**
8:3-4 **ing a golden censer, and much incense was given to**
Him to offer with the prayers of all the saints upon
the golden altar which was before the throne. And the
smoke of the incense went up with the prayers of
the saints out of the hand of the Angel before God.

msg 151

The deepest type of the types in the Old Testament may be the incense altar in Exodus 30....The golden altar of incense must in some way be related to prayer....Actually the incense altar does not refer to our prayer. Rather, it refers to the prayer of Christ, for the altar itself is a type of the person of Christ. It is not a type of Christ's prayer....It signifies Christ praying, Christ interceding.

The individual Christ after His resurrection, and especially after His ascension, has become corporate. Thus, today before God, not only is the individual Christ interceding but the corporate Christ, the Head with the Body, is interceding as well. Christ the Head is interceding in the heavens, and the church the Body is interceding on earth. The intercessor, therefore, is not merely Christ Himself, but is Christ with His Body. If we realize this, we shall see that what is signified by the incense altar is something very deep. (*Life-study of Exodus*, p. 1625)

Today's Reading

According to the [arrangement] of the tabernacle and the outer court, the Ark is the focus. However, in actual practice the center is the incense altar. This indicates that Christ's interceding life is the center of the divine practice, the divine administration....God is not idle: He is a God of purpose. He has a purpose, and He is moving, working, acting, dispensing, administrating. [The arrangement] of the tabernacle is a very accurate and detailed picture of God's administration, God's economy, in this universe.

When we study the incense altar, we are studying the greatest matter in the universe. There is nothing more central than this. ...The Ark in the Holy of Holies is the central government, our heavenly Washington, D.C. The incense altar may be regarded as our heavenly white house. This means that everything is executed, motivated, and carried out from this divine center. The intercession of Christ is God's white house. Christ's interceding life, His prayer life, is the center of God's administration.

On this altar the prayers of the saints are offered to God, and Christ's incense is added to these prayers. When the prayers of the saints ascend to God with the incense of Christ, God executes the policies of His administration.

The prayer life of Christ is the center of God's execution of His government on earth. Revelation 8 indicates this. But some who read chapter eight of Revelation may say, "In Revelation 8 we cannot see Christ's prayer. We can see only the prayers of the saints." The saints, however, are one with Christ. The prayers in Revelation 8 no longer are merely the prayers of the individual Christ, but have become the prayers of the corporate Christ. In the matter of the execution that takes place at the incense altar, the saints truly are one with Christ. Therefore, when we speak...of the prayer life of Christ, we mean the prayer life of the corporate Christ.

As those who are seeking the Lord, we in the recovery both individually and corporately must learn one thing—to pray. We need a praying life. The real praying life is always a life of interceding.

The proper prayer life is a life of praying for others, of interceding for them. We need to pray for the churches throughout the earth and for all the saints. We need to pray for the older ones, the younger ones, and the opposers. Day by day we need to pray not mainly for ourselves, but for others. We need such an interceding life. (*Life-study of Exodus,* pp. 1593-1595, 1602)

Further Reading: Life-study of Exodus, msgs. 147-148; *The Conclusion of the New Testament,* pp. 825-833

Enlightenment and inspiration: _____

_____

_____

Morning Nourishment

Rom. Moreover, in like manner the Spirit also joins in to
8:26-27 help *us* in our weakness, for we do not know for what
we should pray as is fitting, but the Spirit Himself
intercedes for *us* with groanings which cannot be
uttered. But He who searches the hearts knows what
the mind of the Spirit is, because He intercedes
for the saints according to God.

Eph. ...Praying at every time in spirit and watching unto
6:18-19 this in all perseverance and petition concerning all
the saints, and for me, that utterance may be given to
me in the opening of my mouth, to make known in
boldness the mystery of the gospel.

When we come to [the golden altar of incense], our unique
taste, our only interest, is to pray....The prayer we offer at the
incense altar will be intercessory prayers. Whenever we open our
mouth to pray at the incense altar, the prayer that will issue forth
will not be personal, individual prayer. It will be intercessory
prayer. Here we no longer have any interest in ourselves or in our
welfare. Instead of considering ourselves and praying for ourselves, we intercede for others. At that time we shall be in our
experience a real member of Christ, a genuine part of the Body-
Christ, the corporate Christ. Furthermore, that will be the time
when we cooperate with Christ in His ministry of intercession. He
intercedes in a particular way, and we cooperate with Him in His
way of interceding. This means that we carry out His intercession
in our prayers of intercession. This is marvelous! Here we are
truly one with the Lord. (*Life-study of Exodus,* p. 1635)

Today's Reading

[In our experience in the Holy Place], it is very good that we
spend time at the table, the lampstand, and the Ark. But we
should not remain at these places, because they are not our destination. Our destination is the incense altar. Because the incense
altar is our destination, once we arrive there we should remain
and continue there in prayer.

After you have more experience, you will understand more fully what I am saying. Then...you will declare, "After passing through the first altar, the table, the lampstand, and the Ark, I am now at the incense altar interceding for God's interests, for the churches, and for the saints." If we remain at the incense altar, then in Christ and with Christ we shall have something that ascends to God. This is our prayer.

Our prayers represent ourselves. This is true both of the prayers at the first altar and at the second. Whatever we pray will represent us. The kind of prayer we have depends on the kind of person we are, for our prayers reveal our person....None of us is an exception to this principle. The way we pray reveals what we are.

At the first altar we cannot pray intercessory prayers. The reason we cannot pray such prayers at the first altar is that we are not yet the kind of person to offer intercessory prayers. Thus far, you have come only to the first altar. You need to experience it thoroughly and then go on to the table, the lampstand, and the Ark. Not until you reach the second altar can you be the kind of person who is able to offer intercessory prayers. Reaching the incense altar indicates that we have experienced the first altar, the table, the lampstand, and the Ark and have arrived at our destination.

May we all be stirred up to seek such an interceding life so that we may enjoy Christ not only as the table, the lampstand, and the Ark, but also as the incense altar. This incense altar is the turning point of our Christian life. It motivates every aspect of the Christian life to positive action. The prayer of intercession also motivates others to come to Christ at the altar of burnt offering, at the laver, at the table, at the lampstand, and at the Ark in the Holy of Holies. It will motivate a great many saints to seek the riches of Christ until they come to maturity. Therefore, it is extremely important that we intercede with Christ at the incense altar. (*Life-study of Exodus*, pp. 1636-1637, 1606-1607)

Further Reading: Life-study of Exodus, msg. 152; *The Mending Ministry of John,* ch. 15

Enlightenment and inspiration: _____

_____

_____

_____

Morning Nourishment

John
6:56

He who eats My flesh and drinks My blood abides in
Me and I in him.

15:7

If you abide in Me and My words abide in you, ask
whatever you will, and it shall be done for you.

Exo.
30:36-37

And you shall beat some of it very fine, and put some
of it before the Testimony in the Tent of Meeting,
where I will meet with you; it shall be to you most
holy. And the incense which you shall make, you shall
not make for yourselves according to its composition;
it shall be holy to you for Jehovah.

We all need to see three matters. First, when we pray, we should
be in the tabernacle. Second, when we are about to pray, we
should first be satisfied by eating holy food. Third, when we pray,
we should offer incense to God. This means that when we pray, we
should pray in God, we should pray with God within us as our
energizing supply, and we should pray with Christ as the incense.
Then we shall burn incense to God. I believe that if we have this
view concerning prayer, our prayer life will be revolutionized.
May we all see this view and experience such a revolution.

Instead of being occupied in prayer with material needs or personal concerns, we shall pray for the executing of God's purpose, for
the carrying out of the divine administration, and for the dispensing of God's supplying grace. (*Life-study of Exodus*, pp. 1616-1617)

Today's Reading

When we enter into the tabernacle, we should not be empty
within. Rather, we have something to fill us inwardly. We not only
offer the sacrifices to God, but after offering them, we may have a
portion of them to eat. Thus, we have the blood outwardly and the
food, the meat of the offerings, inwardly. The blood of the sacrifice
without opens the way for us to enter into God, and the meat fills
us inwardly. We are not hungry when we come into the tabernacle. No, we are those who have been fully satisfied.

The picture of the tabernacle portrays Christ as the incarnated God who is available for us to enter. This very Christ is also

all the offerings to qualify us by opening the way into God and by filling us inwardly. As a result, we are in God, and God is in us. Therefore, by the time we come to the altar of incense, we are already in God, and God is in us....At the altar in the outer court we experience the offerings, and we have the blood to cleanse us and the meat to fill us inwardly. This qualifies us to enter into the incarnated God, the One who indwells us as our food, as our life supply. Whoever comes to the incense altar is a person who is in God and who has God in him. He is one with God and mingled with Him. What a great matter this is!

Perhaps you have been a Christian for years without realizing that to pray at the incense altar is to pray in God and with God in us. However, those who pray merely in a natural way may be quite far from God, and their prayer may not have the element of God in it. Although they pray to God, they are far away from Him....Whenever we pray we should experientially be in God, and simultaneously, He should be in us. While we are praying to Him, we should be in Him, and He should be praying in us.

According to typology, there is no indication that the incense altar is a place to pray. This is our interpretation. The incense altar is a place to burn incense, and burning the incense typifies praying. How should we pray at the incense altar? Now that we are in God and He is in us, and now that we are at the incense altar, we must burn the incense. But what is this incense? The incense is Christ. Christ is the tabernacle, Christ is the offerings, and Christ is also the incense. Thus, to burn the incense means to pray Christ.

[In Revelation 8:3 and 4, the] Angel is Christ, the One who adds His incense to the prayers of the saints. It is this incense, not the saints' prayers, that causes the smoke to rise. In our prayers we need to have Christ as the incense with the smoke that rises. The point here is that to burn the incense actually means to pray Christ. (*Life-study of Exodus,* pp. 1611-1613)

Further Reading: Life-study of Exodus, msgs. 149, 167

Enlightenment and inspiration: _____

_____

_____

_____

Morning Nourishment

Exo. And Aaron shall burn on it fragrant incense...
30:7, 9 You shall not offer any strange incense on it...
Lev. And Nadab and Abihu, the sons of Aaron, each took
10:1 his censer, and put fire in them and laid incense on it,
and they presented strange fire before Jehovah,
which He had not commanded them.
1 Tim. I desire therefore that men pray in every place, lifting
2:8 up holy hands, without wrath and reasoning.

What God desires is the prayer at the incense altar....This
kind of prayer is intercessory prayer. Whenever we open our
mouths to pray at the incense altar, our prayers will not be for
ourselves. Instead, our prayers will be for God's eternal plan, for
His recovery, for His move, and for all His churches. Our prayer
will indicate where we are and who we are.

When we arrive at our destination, the incense altar, we shall
become intercessors. All day long we shall intercede for others and
for the Lord's interests. This kind of prayer is a fragrant incense to
God. This prayer fulfills God's purpose, satisfies His hunger, and
delights His heart. As we pray in this way, we know that we are
truly one with the Lord. By our prayers of intercession we are one
with Him at the incense altar. (*Life-study of Exodus,* p. 1640)

Today's Reading

When we pray at the incense altar, there will be neither
strange incense nor strange fire in our prayer....Many Christians
pray with strange incense or with strange fire. God wants us to
pray with Christ as our incense. This means that we should pray
with Christ. We should not pray with strange incense....Strange
incense is anything we pray that is not Christ or that is not
related to Christ. In the sight of God, that kind of prayer...is a
prayer with strange incense.

I do not presume to tell you what you should pray for. However,
I can say that you need to ask yourself how much the things you
pray for have to do with Christ. If you consider your prayer life in
this way, you will find out where you are. You may realize that

your prayers concerning your married life have nothing to do with Christ. Thus, those prayers are strange incense.

However, I wish to make it clear that I do not mean we should not pray concerning our personal affairs or for material things that we need. My point here is that we ask ourselves how much our prayers are related to Christ. This question is a test that will reveal whether what we pray is real incense or strange incense.

What is strange fire? According to typology, strange fire is any fire other than that which burns on the altar of burnt offering. The fire that burned on the altar in the outer court came down from the heavens. After coming down from the heavens, that fire burned continually on the altar. The incense must be burned by the fire from the first altar. If you burn incense by any other kind of fire, that will be strange fire.

To have strange fire is to have some kind of motive within us that is natural and that has not been dealt with by the cross. Anything that has not been dealt with by the cross and yet motivates us to pray is strange fire. If we see this, we shall realize that a great many Christians are motivated to pray by natural motives. Their motives have never been touched by the cross. The result is that they pray with strange fire.

To pray something that has nothing to do with Christ is strange incense, and to pray with motives that have not been dealt with by the cross is to have strange fire. In our prayers we may offer strange incense by strange fire. If we see the significance and the seriousness of strange incense and strange fire, we shall confess that much of our prayer in the past has been motivated by our natural motives. We shall also see that much of our prayer has had nothing to do with Christ. Furthermore, we shall realize that we ourselves often have not been in God when we prayed. On the contrary, we were outside of Him....Whether we are in God or outside of God will be indicated by the way we pray. Our prayers always indicate where we are. (*Life-study of Exodus*, pp. 1637-1639)

Further Reading: Life-study of Exodus, msgs. 150, 168

Enlightenment and inspiration: _____

_____

_____

Morning Nourishment

John
15:5

I am the vine; you are the branches....Apart from Me you can do nothing.

1 Cor.
2:14-15

But a soulish man does not receive the things of the Spirit of God, for they are foolishness to him and he is not able to know *them* because they are discerned spiritually. But the spiritual man discerns all things, but he himself is discerned by no one.

The fire that burned on the altar in the outer court was used to burn the incense at the incense altar....The fire indicates that whatever we are needs to be reduced to ashes.

With the sin offerings we can see three things: the blood, the ashes, and the sweet savor ascending to God. The blood and the ashes are related to us, whereas the sweet savor is for God's satisfaction. Thank the Lord that today we have the blood as the sign and assurance that our sin and our trespasses have all been dealt with. We also have the ashes as a sign that we have been crucified, terminated. When we become ashes, we are no longer a natural person. Instead, we are a person who has been crucified, terminated, burned. No longer are we a natural man—we have become a heap of ashes. Nevertheless, for most of us this is true only doctrinally; it is not yet true experientially. Therefore, we need to go on to have the experience of actually being reduced to ashes. (*Life-study of Exodus*, pp. 1627-1629)

Today's Reading

Intercession cannot be made at the first altar; it must be made at the second altar. But...those who pray at the second altar must first be burned to ashes; that is, they must no longer be a natural person. Everyone who would pray at the incense altar must become a heap of ashes.

If we come into the tabernacle, we cannot go directly to the incense altar. As we have already indicated, first we must go to the showbread table, then to the lampstand, and after that to the Ark of the Testimony in the Holy of Holies. Only then shall we be ready to come to intercede at the incense altar.

Our conduct is versus Christ as life (the bread of the presence table, the showbread table). Our sight is versus Christ as our light (the lampstand). Our virtue is versus Christ as our incense to God (the incense altar). Our conduct, our sight, and our virtue together equal our natural being, which is versus Christ as God's testimony (the Ark). If we have become a heap of ashes, will we still have our natural conduct, our natural sight, and our natural virtue? Certainly not....To be reduced to ashes is to be reduced to nothing.

As long as we think that we are something and regard ourselves as something, we are not in the tabernacle. Rather, we are outside the tabernacle. Do you remember what the tabernacle signifies? The tabernacle signifies the incarnated God. Thus, to be in the tabernacle is to be in God. Now we must realize that the requirement for being in God is that we become nothing. We can be in God only if we first become zero. For this reason, I wish to emphasize the fact that if we continue to think that we are something, we are not in God. But when we have become nothing, we are then qualified to be in Him.

Anyone who intercedes at the incense altar has Christ as his incense. He no longer has his natural virtue. With such a person, Christ is everything. Christ is his life supply for proper conduct, Christ is his light for genuine sight, and Christ is his virtue for him to have a sweet fragrance ascending to God. This is the kind of person who can pray at the incense altar.

Nothing that we pray at the first altar, the altar of burnt offering in the outer court, can be an intercession. But whatever we pray at the second altar, the golden altar of incense in the tabernacle, will be an intercession. At the second altar we do not pray much for ourselves. Instead, we pray for God's economy, we pray for God's dispensation, we pray for God's move, we pray for God's recovery, and we pray for the churches and the saints. We intercede in this way spontaneously. (*Life-study of Exodus,* pp. 1629-1632)

Further Reading: Life-study of Exodus, msgs. 151, 169

Enlightenment and inspiration: _____

_____

_____

_____

Hymns, #772

1   Lord, we meet to seek Thy face
     And in one accord to pray;
     We a holy priesthood are,
     Waiting on Thee here today.

       Here together we would pray,
       Touch the highest and the best,
       Till our spirits mingled are
       And Thy Church is built and blest.

2   As true priests we long to be,
     With our spirit sense Thy will,
     Thus to serve before Thee here
     That Thy plan Thou may fulfill.

3   To the holiest place we come,
     Now to touch Thy throne of grace,
     By the inner sense to pray
     And Thy Spirit's flow to trace.

4   From Thy throne of grace to me
     Rivers of Thy grace proceed;
     Thus my spirit is refreshed,
     Helping me in time of need.

5   May our prayers expression give
     To Thy Spirit's mind alone;
     Praying not by our desire,
     But according to Thine own.

6   Though with temporal matters pressed,
     Which we fain would bring to Thee,
     Rather than Thy care to seek,
     We would here Thy channel be.

7   Here we seek Thy list'ning ear,
     May Thy living water flow;
     When Thy grace does satisfy,
     Only then Thy work we'll know.

Composition for prophecy with main point and sub-points: _____

_____

_____

_____

_____

_____

_____

_____

_____

_____

_____

_____

_____

_____

_____

_____

_____

_____

_____

_____

_____

_____

_____

_____

_____

_____

_____

_____

_____

_____

_____

_____

_____

_____

_____

_____

Having a Clear View
concerning the Present Situation
and the Present Need in the Lord's Recovery

Scripture Reading: 1 Tim. 1:3-4; Acts 1:14; Eph. 4:11-14; Titus 3:10; Rom. 16:17; Acts 26:19

Day 1

I. **We need to see that teaching different things other than the unique ministry of God's economy creates division; the ministry of the New Testament, which is the ministry of the new covenant, is uniquely one universally (1 Tim. 1:3-4; Acts 1:17, 25; 2 Cor. 3:6, 8-9; 4:1; 1 Tim. 1:12):**

A. Any teaching other than the unique teaching of God's economy is considered by the apostles as a different teaching (vv. 3-4).

B. The ministry of the New Testament is according to the apostles' teaching, the teaching of God's New Testament economy, for the building up of the Body of Christ to consummate the New Jerusalem (2 Cor. 3:6; Eph. 3:9-10; 4:11-13).

C. The New Testament ministry is uniquely one and corporate, but because this ministry is the service of the Body of Christ and because the Body has many members, every member has its own personal ministry (1 Tim. 1:12; 2 Tim. 4:5).

D. Although the ministers are many, all these ministers have only one corporate ministry, which is the New Testament ministry (1 Cor. 16:10; 2 Cor. 4:1).

Day 2

E. To teach differently tears down God's building and annuls God's entire economy; only one kind of ministry builds up and never divides—this is the unique ministry of God's economy (1 Tim. 6:3-4).

F. The different teachings of the dissenting ones are winds used by God's enemy to distract His people and carry them away from His economy; these different teachings are the major source of the church's decline, degradation, and deterioration (Eph. 4:14; 1 Tim. 1:3-7; 6:3-5, 20-21).

G. The basic factor of all the divisions, their very root, is different ministries; all the troubles, divisions, and confusions come from the one source of the tolerance of different ministries (2 Cor. 11:2-3):

   1. "If we are not watchful, if we are careless, in one way or another the enemy would creepingly use some means, some ways, to bring in different ministries. Such a thing would end the Lord's recovery" (*Elders' Training, Book 1: The Ministry of the New Testament,* p. 16).

   2. "If you could take away all the different ministries and leave only the unique ministry of the New Testament, all the denominations, all the different groups, and all the divisions would disappear…If we carry out something new, something different, something other than this unique ministry, we will be through as far as the Lord's recovery is concerned. Actually, the Lord's recovery is to bring us back to the unique ministry of the New Testament" (pp. 70-71).

Day 3   H. The saints who have been raised up by this ministry have a taste for this ministry, and this taste is the controlling factor in the Lord's recovery; those who have been raised up by this ministry will reject a taste that is contrary to it; this means that if you speak something contrary to the taste of the Lord's recovery, your speaking will be rejected and you will suffer loss (1 Pet. 2:3).

II. **The problem of rebellion among us comes out of certain divisive factors:**

A. The intention to do an extra work within the unique work of the Lord's recovery is a divisive factor; in the Lord's recovery there is one unique work for the accomplishment of God's eternal economy to build up the Body of Christ (see *Life-study of 1 & 2 Samuel,* pp. 64-65, and *Further Consideration of the Eldership, the Region of Work, and the Care for the Body of Christ,* pp. 18-19).

B. The tendency to keep separate territories is a divisive

factor; we should work for the Lord within His measure (2 Cor. 10:13-16), but we should not consider what the Lord has measured to us as our particular territory.

C. The way of not having one's work mingled with others' work is a divisive factor; Peter's work for the Lord and Paul's were all for the one Body of Christ without any distinction or separation (1 Cor. 1:12; Acts 15:2, 4; 21:17-20a).

D. The hidden expectation of being a prominent figure in the Lord's work is a divisive factor (3 John 9; cf. Acts 15:39).

E. The negligence regarding the keeping of the one accord in the Lord's recovery is a divisive factor (1:14; 2:42, 46; Eph. 4:3).

F. Many of the dissenting accusations of the rebellious, divisive, and factious persons today are the same accusations of Satan (Rev. 12:10-11) in the previous turmoil among us (see *Elders' Training, Book 10: The Eldership and the God-ordained Way (2)*, pp. 93-112, and *The Practice of the Church Life according to the God-ordained Way*, pp. 19-48).

Day 4   III. **The way to deal with any present rebellious and divisive situation is to pay full attention to the truth concerning the church as the Body of Christ and as the house and kingdom of God (Eph. 4:15-16; 1 Tim. 3:15; Rom. 14:17), to keep the truth at any cost (2 John 1-2; 3 John 3-4), to reject any kind of division (1 Cor. 1:10), to stand against any wind of teaching and any spreading of spiritual death (Eph. 4:14; 2 Tim. 2:16-17), and to separate ourselves from the contagious ones—exercising to quarantine (Titus 3:10; Rom. 16:17):**

A. In today's situation it is not a matter of being right or wrong; it is a matter of whether we are divisive or not (1 Cor. 1:10-13; cf. Gen. 2:9).

B. Being neutral does not build up (2 Cor. 13:8, 10) but destroys the Body of Christ; we need to practice the Body life by receiving the believers and turning away from those who make divisions (Rom. 14:1-3; 16:17).

C. To keep the truth we need to overcome personal affection with the vow of a Nazarite; we need to put aside our natural relationships and practice the truth of the Body (Num. 6:1-9; cf. Lev. 10:6-7; Exo. 32:25-29; Deut. 33:8-9).

D. We need to be inoculators, those who are full of life and constituted with the truth, to inoculate others against the decline of the church (2 Tim. 2:1-15; 1 John 5:16a; Titus 1:9).

E. We need to stand on the unique ground of the local churches of God and pay the price to enter into the practice and intrinsic significance of blending for the oneness and reality of the Body of Christ (1 Cor. 1:1-2, 9-13; 12:24; Eph. 4:3-6).

Day 5   IV. **We must receive the Lord's mercy to be His overcomers who bring in a new revival to turn the age in the Lord's present recovery by arriving at the highest peak of the divine revelation, by living the life of a God-man, and by shepherding people according to God in the vital groups for the building up of the Body of Christ, the preparation of the bride of Christ:**

A. We can enter into a new revival by arriving at the highest peak of the divine revelation through the ministry of the age; the particular recovery and work that God is doing in one age is the ministry of that age; in every age there is the vision of that age, and we have to serve God according to the vision of the age (Prov. 29:18; Acts 26:19; Eph. 1:17; 3:9):

1. In order for us to serve God today, our vision must extend all the way from the first vision of Adam in Genesis to the ultimate vision of John in Revelation; today we can be in one accord because we have only one vision—an up-to-date, all-inheriting vision, the vision of God's eternal economy.

2. God's eternal economy is to make man the same as He is in life and nature but not in the Godhead and to make Himself one with man and man one with Him, thus to be enlarged and expanded in His expression, that all His divine attributes may be expressed in human virtues (1 Tim. 1:3-4).

3. "I hope that the saints...will see this revelation and then rise up to pray that God would give us a new revival—a revival which has never been recorded in history" (*Life-study of 1 & 2 Chronicles,* p. 15).

4. "We have to learn the high peaks of God's present revelation and learn to speak these things...I would encourage all of us to pick up this high commission: to go out with the high peaks of the divine revelation and with God's up-to-date vision to move with God for His high peaks of the divine revelation that will consummate His eternal economy" (*The Triune God's Revelation and His Move,* p. 98).

Day 6

B. If we practice living the life of a God-man, which is the reality of the Body of Christ, a corporate model will be built up, a model living in the economy of God; this model will be the greatest revival in the history of the church to bring the Lord back:

1. The reality of the Body of Christ is a corporate living, a mingling living, in the eternal union of the regenerated, transformed, and glorified tripartite God-men with the Triune God in the resurrection of Christ (cf. Lev. 2:4-5).

2. "If among us there is, if not in full at least in part, such a living, the reality of the Body of Christ is among us. This is the high peak of the recovery in the local churches like Mount Zion in the city of Jerusalem. Such a mingling living as the reality of the Body of Christ will consummate ultimately in the New Jerusalem in the new heaven and new earth as God's

increase and expression for eternity" (*The Practical Points concerning Blending,* p. 37).

3. "We should all declare that we want to live the life of a God-man. Eventually, the God-men will be the victors, the overcomers, the Zion within Jerusalem. This will bring in a new revival which has never been seen in history, and this will end this age" (*Life-study of 1 & 2 Chronicles,* p. 28).

C. We need to coordinate with Christ in His heavenly ministry to shepherd people according to God in the vital groups for the fulfillment of the economy of God to build up the Body of Christ (1 Pet. 5:4; 2:25; Acts 20:28):

1. "I hope that there will be a genuine revival among us by our receiving this burden of shepherding. If all the churches receive this teaching to participate in Christ's wonderful shepherding, there will be a big revival in the recovery" (*The Vital Groups,* p. 40).

2. "I hope that we would pray, 'Lord, I want to be revived. From today I want to be a shepherd. I want to go to feed people, to shepherd people, and to flock people together'" (*Crystallization-study of the Gospel of John,* p. 137).

3. "If we practice these things, there will be a real revival in the Lord's recovery. We must be shepherds with the loving and forgiving heart of our Father God in His divinity and the shepherding and finding spirit of our Savior Christ in His humanity. We also must have the heavenly vision of all the divine and mystical teachings of Christ. Shepherding and teaching are the obligation of the vital groups and the basic way ordained by God to build up the Body of Christ consummating the New Jerusalem" (*The Vital Groups,* pp. 55-56).

Morning Nourishment

2 Cor. **Who has also made us sufficient as ministers of a**
3:6 **new covenant, *ministers* not of the letter but of the**
Spirit; for the letter kills, but the Spirit gives life.
4:1 **Therefore having this ministry as we have been**
shown mercy, we do not lose heart.

In the entire universe there have been only two ministries. In 2 Corinthians 3 the ministry of the old covenant is referred to as "the ministry of death" and "the ministry of condemnation" (vv. 7, 9). The ministry of the old covenant did only two things: it condemned people and put people to death. But the new covenant and the new ministry based on the new covenant is a ministry of the Spirit and of righteousness, that is, of justification (vv. 8, 9)....Thus, we may say that the ministry of the old covenant was a ministry of death and condemnation, and the ministry of the new covenant is a ministry of life and justification. (*The Ministry of the New Testament and the Teaching and Fellowship of the Apostles,* pp. 9-10)

Today's Reading

We all need to be clear that the ministry of the New Testament, which is the ministry of the new covenant, is uniquely one universally.

The unique ministry of the New Testament comprises all the works (ministries) of all the apostles, the ministers of the new covenant. In 2 Corinthians 3 the plural *ministers* is used clearly in verse 6, and the singular *ministry* is used in verses 8 and 9. Then, in the first verse of chapter four Paul said, "Therefore having this ministry as we have been shown mercy, we do not lose heart."...*We* here includes not only Paul but all the New Testament ministers. All this indicates that there is one new covenant ministry of many new covenant ministers.

The first of the new covenant ministers were the twelve apostles. In Acts 1:17 and 25 Peter used the term *this ministry.* That ministry was the ministry of the twelve apostles, who were the first twelve New Testament ministers....After the twelve apostles, many ministers, including Paul, Barnabas, and many others, entered into the ministry. Although the ministers were many, all these many ministers had only one ministry.

In 2 Timothy 4:5 Paul charged Timothy to fully accomplish his ministry....This was Timothy's personal ministry, but this personal ministry was a part of the corporate ministry, "this ministry," the unique ministry of the New Testament.

The work of the New Testament ministry is to accomplish God's New Testament economy concerning the church (Eph. 3:9-10) in the building up of the Body of Christ. Ephesians 4:12 says that all the saints need to be perfected "unto the work of the ministry." This means that hundreds and even thousands of saints can be perfected unto the work of the ministry....In Ephesians 4:12 the phrase *unto the building up of the Body of Christ* appears in apposition to *unto the work of the ministry.* This indicates clearly that to do the work of the ministry is to build up the Body of Christ.

In recent years some of the dissenting ones have said that they accept all ministries. In saying "all ministries" they seem to have the concept that the new covenant has many ministries. However, this is wrong. Since there is only one new covenant, how could there be many new covenant ministries? Many workers may have a part in constructing a building, but they do not carry out many different works. Rather, they carry out only one work. That one work is not done according to anyone's opinion but is carried out under one superintendent, one master builder (1 Cor. 3:10), and according to the unique copy of the blueprint. The one blueprint eliminates all opinions. Every part of the work must be done according to the one blueprint and under the leadership of the one master builder. In this way all the workers carry out only one building work. (*The Ministry of the New Testament and the Teaching and Fellowship of the Apostles,* pp. 9-12)

Further Reading: The Ministry of the New Testament and the Teaching and Fellowship of the Apostles, ch. 1

Enlightenment and inspiration: _____
_____
_____
_____

Morning Nourishment

1 Tim. **Even as I exhorted you, when I was going into Mac-**
1:3-4 **edonia, to remain in Ephesus in order that you**
might charge certain ones not to teach different
things,…which produce questionings rather than
God's economy, which is in faith.

The many divisions and confusions among the Christians today all come from one source—a ministry.…All the different kinds of Christian groups come out of different ministries. A ministry is mainly a teaching,…[and] a teaching always issues in something.

Paul wrote 1 Timothy in the midst of a confusing environment…[as] an inoculation. Poison after poison was injected into the Christian church while the church was going on. At the conclusion of his writing ministry, Paul wrote 1 Timothy to inoculate the church against all these poisons. In the opening word of this Epistle, however, Paul did not write in a way that we would think to be so serious: "Even as I exhorted you, when I was going into Macedonia, to remain in Ephesus in order that you might charge certain ones not to teach different things" (1:3). This phrase "not to teach different things" seems so simple. If you merely read this phrase, you will not sense the seriousness of different teaching. We may not think that this is serious, but actually it is more than serious. It kills people to teach differently. To teach differently tears down God's building and annuls God's entire economy. We all must realize that even a small amount of teaching in a different way destroys the recovery. There is a proverb which says, "One sentence can build up the nation and one sentence can destroy the entire nation." You do not need to give an entire message. Just by speaking one sentence which conveys your kind of concept tears down everything. We must realize that ministry is "terrible." Your speaking can build up or destroy. It is possible that your speaking destroys, kills, and annuls. (*Elders' Training, Book 3: The Way to Carry out the Vision,* pp. 41-43)

Today's Reading

We all must realize that, generally speaking, the different

denominations do not teach anything wrong. They have all tried and endeavored to teach the right things, the scriptural things. Eventually, however, the Body of Christ has been cut into pieces.

We want the teaching which teaches God's economy. Now we can understand Paul's charge in 1 Corinthians to speak the same thing (1:10). What same thing should we speak? Should we speak Bible teaching, how to meet, the way to baptize, the way to edify the saints, the way to help people to be spiritual, or the way to render much help to the Christians that they may grow in life? These are right things to teach. Something from the Bible such as evangelism is altogether right. However, if you do these things and teach them apart from God's economy, you are divisive. You are divisive in right things, in scriptural things, not in wrong things, heathen things, or pagan things....Whatever you teach should not be measured by whether it is wrong or right. It must be measured by whether it is divisive or not. Only one kind of ministry builds up and never divides—this is the unique ministry of God's economy. We must be reminded that Paul left Timothy in Ephesus with a charge to tell certain ones not to teach different things and that what they teach should be related to God's economy. (*Elders' Training, Book 3: The Way to Carry out the Vision,* pp. 44-46)

We need to see this principle throughout the entire Christian era. All the troubles, divisions, and confusions came from the one source of the tolerance of different ministries. Many Christian teachers have known the peril of different ministries; nevertheless, they have tolerated them. There has been a tolerance of different ministries. In the Lord's recovery,...we must be on the alert. Such a peril is ahead of us. If we are not watchful, if we are careless, in one way or another the enemy would creepingly use some means, some ways, to bring in different ministries. Such a thing would end the Lord's recovery. (*Elders' Training, Book 1: The Ministry of the New Testament,* pp. 15-16)

Further Reading: Elders' Training, Book 3: The Way to Carry Out the Vision, ch. 4

Enlightenment and inspiration: _____

_____

_____

_____

Morning Nourishment

2 Cor. 10:13	But we will not boast beyond *our* measure but according to the measure of the rule which the God of measure has apportioned to us, to reach even as far as you.
1 Pet. 2:3	If you have tasted that the Lord is good.

The Lord's recovery also has a taste for the ministry that has built up the recovery over the years....Those who have been raised with this taste will reject a taste that is contrary to it.

Brothers who teach differently actually are trying to bring in a foreign element; they are trying to wedge in a foreign particle into the "body" of the recovery. The recovery will not accept any kind of foreign element....The reason is that the saints have their taste.

Although the recovery is not controlled by any person, there is a controlling factor in the Lord's recovery, and this factor is the taste in the recovery. The recovery has a particular taste because it has a certain life that came from its birth....This taste is the controlling factor in the Lord's recovery. No one can overthrow this controlling factor. If you try to overthrow it, you yourself will be overthrown,...separated from the Lord's recovery. (*Elders' Training, Book 3: The Way to Carry out the Vision*, pp. 125-126)

Today's Reading

The present problem among us came out of something which was hidden in the past....In the recovery there is a definite work which is for the building up of the local churches unto the building up of the universal Body of Christ....But among us, there was a case of someone who wanted to do an extra work within the work. This person would not leave the recovery or give up the church life. Instead, he insisted on having a particular work of his own, by his own effort, within the recovery. This was a divisive factor.

Another hidden divisive factor is the tendency to keep separate territories. The Lord's work and move for the accomplishment of God's eternal economy is uniquely one. If we consider any region in which we are participating in the Lord's unique work as our particular territory, this will be a cause or a factor of division.... We should work for the Lord within His measure (2 Cor. 10:13-16), but we should not consider what the Lord has measured to us as our particular territory. Our local work in our region should be for the Lord's universal Body. In the New Testament we cannot see such a thing as jurisdiction in the Lord's work.

In the past there was the hidden factor of working in a way of not having one's work mingled with others' work. The New Testament unveils to us that Peter's...and Paul's [work for the Lord]... were all for the one Body of Christ, without any distinction or separation. Rather, they were one in the carrying out of God's New Testament economy. The effect of Peter's work was realized in Corinth (1 Cor. 1:12), and Paul did go to Jerusalem to fellowship with the apostles and elders there (Acts 15:2, 4; 21:17-20a). This kind of fellowship, like the blood circulation of our physical body, helps the Body of Christ in the circulation of the divine life. It mingles the different pieces of our work for the Lord's recovery into one move. If our work is void of this kind of fellowship, this may develop into another factor of division.

There was also the hidden expectation of being a prominent figure in the Lord's work. We cannot deny that this "gopher" of ambition was among us.

Another great divisive factor in the past has been the negligence regarding the keeping of the one accord in the Lord's recovery. In the elders' training in February 1986, my burden was to ask the elders to take care of the one accord in the Lord's recovery.

I believe that this turmoil is initiated by Satan, the evil one, the enemy (Matt. 13:19, 28). It is something from the realm of darkness to destroy the ministry and to shut the door to the new way. (*Elders' Training, Book 10: The Eldership and the God-ordained Way (2),* pp. 18-20, 22-23)

Further Reading: Elders' Training, Book 10: The Eldership and the God-ordained Way (2), ch. 1; *Life-study of 1 & 2 Samuel,* msg. 10; *Further Consideration of the Eldership, the Region of Work, and the Care for the Body of Christ,* ch. 1; *Elders' Training, Book 3: The Way to Carry Out the Vision,* ch. 12

Enlightenment and inspiration: _____

_____

_____

_____

Morning Nourishment

1 Cor. Now I beseech you, brothers, through the name of our
1:10 Lord Jesus Christ, that you all speak the same thing
and *that* there be no divisions among you, but *that* you
be attuned in the same mind and in the same opinion.
11:19 For there must even be parties among you, that those
who are approved may become manifest among you.

In recent years, certain ones left us and formed divisions. It
seems that the leaders among them are doing nothing but trav-
eling from place to place in order to create and strengthen such
divisions. Division has become a thing that motivates and ener-
gizes them. The goal of their activity is to separate the saints
from the enjoyment of the New Testament ministry. Their intention is to poison the saints in order to deaden them, cool them
down, and cause them to have doubts about the Lord's recovery.
The main factor with these ones is that they have left the church
and joined themselves to the "demon" of division.

I have published a book called *The Fermentation of the Present Rebellion,* presenting the whole story, fully documented.
That book concludes by saying that we need to "reject any kind
of division (1 Cor. 1:10), to stand against any wind of teaching
and any spreading of spiritual death (Eph. 4:14; 2 Tim. 2:16-17),
and to separate ourselves from the contagious ones—exercising
to quarantine" (Titus 3:10; Rom. 16:17). Some, however, have not
agreed to quarantine these ones and have embraced division.
(*Life-study of Judges,* p. 40)

Today's Reading

First Corinthians 11:19 says that divisions are unavoidable
that the approved ones might be made manifest. The kind of turmoil and rebellion that we are now experiencing always sifts the
congregation. In such a situation, some are sifted and some are
manifested as being approved.

Most people pay their attention to the matter of being right
or wrong. However, in today's situation, it is not a matter of right
or wrong; it is a matter of whether we are divisive or not.

Being neutral does not build up (2 Cor. 13:8, 10) but destroys the Body of Christ. Being neutral may come out of a good heart, but it is the wrong way.

To keep the truth, we need to overcome personal affection with the vow of a Nazarite. In Numbers 6:6-7, the Nazarites were charged not to be contaminated by any kind of death, even by the death of their blood relatives. Therefore, we must be careful about anyone who is "dying" or who is spreading death. If we realize that one who is near us is "dying" or is spreading death, we must keep ourselves away. Otherwise, if we remain near such a person, we will be contaminated by the germs of death. This will nullify our vow, and we will have to begin our vow over again (Num. 6:9-12). In some cases, to avoid the contagion of death, we need to overcome our personal affection, especially for those with whom we are well-acquainted. Leviticus 10:6-7, Exodus 32:25-29, and Deuteronomy 33:8-9 all stress the need of the overcoming of our personal affection in the service of our priesthood. Both Exodus 32:25-29 and Deuteronomy 33:8-9 tell us that when the children of Israel worshipped the golden calf, offending the Lord to the uttermost, Moses spoke the word asking all the Levites to kill their relatives and those who were close to them. They obeyed, and as a result they obtained the priesthood. The Urim and Thummim were with them, meaning that they had the revelation; they had the vision of the Lord's oracle because of their faithfulness to God's person. God hates to see His people worship anyone besides Him. So, He demands that His faithful people "kill" all the idol worshippers. One of these worshippers might be our father, and one might be our sister. In order to be faithful to the Lord, we must overcome our personal affection. (*Elders' Training, Book 10: The Eldership and the God-ordained Way (2)*, pp. 110-111)

Further Reading: Elders' Training, Book 10: The Eldership and the God-ordained Way (2), ch. 6; *The Divine and Mystical Realm*, ch. 6

Enlightenment and inspiration: _____

_____

_____

_____

Morning Nourishment

Acts **Therefore, King Agrippa, I was not disobedient to**
26:19 **the heavenly vision.**

Eph. **And to enlighten all** *that they may see* **what the econ-**
3:9 **omy of the mystery is, which throughout the ages**
  has been hidden in God, who created all things.

Prov. **Where there is no vision, the people cast off restraint...**
29:18

From the time the apostle John completed the book of Revelation until today, nineteen centuries have passed. During the past nineteen hundred years, countless numbers of Christians have been serving God....Some Christians are serving according to the vision revealed in the New Testament Gospels, which has to do only with the earthly ministry of Jesus. Some serve without any vision at all. In order to serve God according to the up-to-date vision, we need to come up to the level of Paul's very last Epistles. In fact, we need to come up to the level of the epistles to the seven churches in Revelation as well as the revelation which covers all the ages, including the kingdom, the new heaven and new earth, and the ultimate consummation of the church—the New Jerusalem. Simply put, in order for us to serve God today, our vision must extend all the way from the first vision of Adam in Genesis to the ultimate vision of the manifestation of the church, the New Jerusalem. This and this alone is the complete vision. It is not until today that this vision has been fully opened to us.

I wish that all the brothers and sisters would have an enlarged and far-reaching view. I hope they will realize that all the books that we have put out cover the entire spectrum from the first scene to the last scene. We are not serving God based on the first few scenes alone. We are serving God according to the last scene which includes all the previous scenes. (*The Vision of the Age*, pp. 47-49)

Today's Reading

We should serve God according to the entire spectrum, from the first scene of Adam to the last scene in Revelation....The goal of all our services, including preaching the gospel and edifying the believers, must be ultimately consummated in the New Jerusalem.

You are not following a man; rather, you are standing with the Lord's ministry. You are following a vision, a vision that matches the age, a vision that inherits all that was in the past and a vision that is all-inclusive. It is up to date, and yet it builds on the past. If you remain in the book of Acts, you may have inherited everything prior to that time, but you are not up to date. Today as we stand here and ponder the revelations unveiled in the Lord's recovery, as we read the publications that are released among us, we can see that they cover everything from the church to God's economy to the New Jerusalem in the new heaven and new earth. This is a bountiful and all-sufficient vision. If you remain in this vision, you are serving according to the vision.

Where there is no vision, the people cast off restraint, because there is no one accord. It is true that many people love the Lord and serve God, but everyone has his opinion and his own vision. As a result, there is no way to have the one accord. This is the reason that Christianity has become so weak. God's people are divided and split apart. There are divisions everywhere. Although everyone says that he loves the Lord, there is no clear vision, and men are "carried about by every wind" (Eph. 4:14).

Today we can be in one accord because we have only one vision and one view. We are all in this up-to-date, all-inheriting vision. We have only one viewpoint. We speak the same thing with one heart, one mouth, one voice, and one tone, serving the Lord together. The result is a power that will become our strong morale and our impact. This is our strength. Once the Lord's recovery possesses this power, there will be the glory of increase and multiplication. Today our situation is not yet to that point; it is not yet at the peak. Although we do not have many major contentions, we do have some small complaints and criticisms. These things lower our morale. (*The Vision of the Age*, pp. 49, 52-54)

Further Reading: The Vision of the Age, chs. 2-3; The Practical Points concerning Blending, ch. 2; The High Peak of the Vision and the Reality of the Body of Christ, chs. 1-2

Enlightenment and inspiration: _____

_____
_____
_____

Morning Nourishment

1 Pet.	**Shepherd the flock of God among you, overseeing**
5:2-4	**not under compulsion but willingly, according to God; not by seeking gain through base means but eagerly...and when the Chief Shepherd is manifested, you will receive the unfading crown of glory.**
2:25	**For you were like sheep being led astray, but you have now returned to the Shepherd and Overseer of your souls.**

I hope that there will be a genuine revival among us by our receiving this burden of shepherding. If all the churches receive this teaching to participate in Christ's wonderful shepherding, there will be a big revival in the recovery. In the past we did much speaking and teaching with very little shepherding. Shepherding and teaching should be like two feet for our move with the Lord. Our shepherding should always be with teaching, and our teaching should always be with shepherding. (*The Vital Groups,* p. 40)

Today's Reading

Shepherding and teaching are the obligation of the vital groups. If we do not do this, we owe something to the Lord, to the saints, and to all the sinners on this earth (Rom. 1:14). Shepherding...is the basic way ordained by God in the building up of the Body of Christ to consummate His eternal goal—the New Jerusalem.

Christ came to seek the sinners that they might have His life and have it abundantly, so we should not go out to reach people in a shallow and empty way. We should go out full of the divine life so that people may have Christ's life through us. We must be filled to the brim with Christ's life so that His life flows out of us to be dispensed into others....In this sense, we become Christ.

We also need to teach the divine truths to people to strengthen our shepherding and reach its goal....Our going out as Christ to give people life and truth will attract and convince them. We need to be discipled to be such a Christ....This is my burden.

If we practice these things, there will be a real revival in the Lord's recovery. We must be shepherds with the loving and forgiving heart of our Father God in His divinity and the shepherding and finding spirit of our Savior Christ in His humanity. We also must have the heavenly vision of all the divine and mystical teachings of Christ. Shepherding and teaching are the obligation of the vital groups and the basic way ordained by God to build up the Body of Christ consummating the New Jerusalem. (*The Vital Groups*, pp. 51, 55-56)

Since we have seen such a high peak of the divine revelation, we need to put [it] into practice....Our practice will have a success, and that success will be a new revival—the highest revival, and probably the last revival before the Lord's coming back....We need a corporate model, a Body, a people who live the life of a God-man.

This should be and this must be our church practice from today onward. If not, we are practicing something in vain. Our practice is not merely to have a church life in which everything is according to the Bible, a church life in which we baptize people by immersion, forsake the denominations, practice head covering, and have the Lord's table, absolutely according to the Bible. Some have come into the recovery because of these practices. They appreciate our family life, the church meetings, and the way we train our young people. However, these things should not be the goal of our practice. The goal of our practice should be to live the life of a God-man. This is the goal we should reach.

A vital group is a group of this kind of people. The vital groups should not be practiced as a formality; they should be groups of people who live such a life. Our living the life of a God-man will save people, edify others, and build up the local churches even to the building up of the Body of Christ.

If we practice what we have heard, spontaneously a model will be built up. This model will be the greatest revival in the history of the church. I believe that this revival will bring the Lord back. (*Living a Life according to the High Peak of God's Revelation*, pp. 39-41)

Further Reading: The Vital Groups, msg. 6; *Living a Life according to the High Peak of God's Revelation*, chs. 4-5

Enlightenment and inspiration: _____

_____

_____

_____

What Miracle! What Mystery!

1   What miracle! What mystery!
That God and man should blended be!
God became man to make man God,
Untraceable economy!
From His good pleasure, heart's desire,
His highest goal attained will be.
From His good pleasure, heart's desire,
His highest goal attained will be.

2   Flesh He became, the first God-man,
His pleasure that I God may be:
In life and nature I'm God's kind,
Though Godhead's His exclusively.
His attributes my virtues are;
His glorious image shines through me.
His attributes my virtues are;
His glorious image shines through me.

3   No longer I alone that live,
But God together lives with me.
Built with the saints in the Triune God,
His universal house we'll be,
And His organic Body we
For His expression corp'rately.
And His organic Body we
For His expression corp'rately.

4   Jerusalem, the ultimate,
Of visions the totality;
The Triune God, tripartite man—
A loving pair eternally—
As man yet God they coinhere,
A mutual dwelling place to be;
God's glory in humanity
Shines forth in splendor radiantly!

*Composition for prophecy with main point and
sub-points:* _____
_____
_____
_____
_____
_____
_____
_____
_____
_____
_____
_____
_____
_____
_____
_____
_____
_____
_____
_____
_____
_____
_____
_____
_____
_____
_____
_____
_____
_____
_____
_____

Reading Schedule for the Recovery Version of the Old Testament with Footnotes

Wk.	Lord's Day	Monday	Tuesday	Wednesday	Thursday	Friday	Saturday
1	Gen 1:1-5	1:6-23	1:24-31	2:1-9	2:10-25	3:1-13	3:14-24
2	4:1-26	5:1-32	6:1-22	7:1—8:3	8:4-22	9:1-29	10:1-32
3	11:1-32	12:1-20	13:1-18	14:1-24	15:1-21	16:1-16	17:1-27
4	18:1-33	19:1-38	20:1-18	21:1-34	22:1-24	23:1—24:27	24:28-67
5	25:1-34	26:1-35	27:1-46	28:1-22	29:1-35	30:1-43	31:1-55
6	32:1-32	33:1—34:31	35:1-29	36:1-43	37:1-36	38:1—39:23	40:1—41:13
7	41:14-57	42:1-38	43:1-34	44:1-34	45:1-28	46:1-34	47:1-31
8	48:1-22	49:1-15	49:16-33	50:1-26	Exo 1:1-22	2:1-25	3:1-22
9	4:1-31	5:1-23	6:1-30	7:1-25	8:1-32	9:1-35	10:1-29
10	11:1-10	12:1-14	12:15-36	12:37-51	13:1-22	14:1-31	15:1-27
11	16:1-36	17:1-16	18:1-27	19:1-25	20:1-26	21:1-36	22:1-31
12	23:1-33	24:1-18	25:1-22	25:23-40	26:1-14	26:15-37	27:1-21
13	28:1-21	28:22-43	29:1-21	29:22-46	30:1-10	30:11-38	31:1-17
14	31:18—32:35	33:1-23	34:1-35	35:1-35	36:1-38	37:1-29	38:1-31
15	39:1-43	40:1-38	Lev 1:1-17	2:1-16	3:1-17	4:1-35	5:1-19
16	6:1-30	7:1-38	8:1-36	9:1-24	10:1-20	11:1-47	12:1-8
17	13:1-28	13:29-59	14:1-18	14:19-32	14:33-57	15:1-33	16:1-17
18	16:18-34	17:1-16	18:1-30	19:1-37	20:1-27	21:1-24	22:1-33
19	23:1-22	23:23-44	24:1-23	25:1-23	25:24-55	26:1-24	26:25-46
20	27:1-34	Num 1:1-54	2:1-34	3:1-51	4:1-49	5:1-31	6:1-27
21	7:1-41	7:42-88	7:89—8:26	9:1-23	10:1-36	11:1-35	12:1—13:33
22	14:1-45	15:1-41	16:1-50	17:1—18:7	18:8-32	19:1-22	20:1-29
23	21:1-35	22:1-41	23:1-30	24:1-25	25:1-18	26:1-65	27:1-23
24	28:1-31	29:1-40	30:1—31:24	31:25-54	32:1-42	33:1-56	34:1-29
25	35:1-34	36:1-13	Deut 1:1-46	2:1-37	3:1-29	4:1-49	5:1-33
26	6:1—7:26	8:1-20	9:1-29	10:1-22	11:1-32	12:1-32	13:1—14:21

Reading Schedule for the Recovery Version of the Old Testament with Footnotes

Wk.	Lord's Day	Monday	Tuesday	Wednesday	Thursday	Friday	Saturday
27	☐ 14:22—15:23	☐ 16:1-22	☐ 17:1—18:8	☐ 18:9—19:21	☐ 20:1—21:17	☐ 21:18—22:30	☐ 23:1-25
28	☐ 24:1-22	☐ 25:1-19	☐ 26:1-19	☐ 27:1-26	☐ 28:1-68	☐ 29:1-29	☐ 30:1—31:29
29	☐ 31:30—32:52	☐ 33:1-29	☐ 34:1-12	☐ Josh 1:1-18	☐ 2:1-24	☐ 3:1-17	☐ 4:1-24
30	☐ 5:1-15	☐ 6:1-27	☐ 7:1-26	☐ 8:1-35	☐ 9:1-27	☐ 10:1-43	☐ 11:1—12:24
31	☐ 13:1-33	☐ 14:1—15:63	☐ 16:1—18:28	☐ 19:1-51	☐ 20:1—21:45	☐ 22:1-34	☐ 23:1—24:33
32	☐ Judg 1:1-36	☐ 2:1-23	☐ 3:1-31	☐ 4:1-24	☐ 5:1-31	☐ 6:1-40	☐ 7:1-25
33	☐ 8:1-35	☐ 9:1-57	☐ 10:1—11:40	☐ 12:1—13:25	☐ 14:1—15:20	☐ 16:1-31	☐ 17:1—18:31
34	☐ 19:1-30	☐ 20:1-48	☐ 21:1-25	☐ Ruth 1:1-22	☐ 2:1-23	☐ 3:1-18	☐ 4:1-22
35	☐ 1 Sam 1:1-28	☐ 2:1-36	☐ 3:1—4:22	☐ 5:1—6:21	☐ 7:1—8:22	☐ 9:1-27	☐ 10:1—11:15
36	☐ 12:1—13:23	☐ 14:1-52	☐ 15:1-35	☐ 16:1-23	☐ 17:1-58	☐ 18:1-30	☐ 19:1-24
37	☐ 20:1-42	☐ 21:1—22:23	☐ 23:1—24:22	☐ 25:1-44	☐ 26:1-25	☐ 27:1—28:25	☐ 29:1—30:31
38	☐ 31:1-13	☐ 2 Sam 1:1-27	☐ 2:1-32	☐ 3:1-39	☐ 4:1—5:25	☐ 6:1-23	☐ 7:1-29
39	☐ 8:1—9:13	☐ 10:1—11:27	☐ 12:1-31	☐ 13:1-39	☐ 14:1-33	☐ 15:1—16:23	☐ 17:1—18:33
40	☐ 19:1-43	☐ 20:1—21:22	☐ 22:1-51	☐ 23:1-39	☐ 24:1-25	☐ 1 Kings 1:1-19	☐ 1:20-53
41	☐ 2:1-46	☐ 3:1-28	☐ 4:1-34	☐ 5:1—6:38	☐ 7:1-22	☐ 7:23-51	☐ 8:1-36
42	☐ 8:37-66	☐ 9:1-28	☐ 10:1-29	☐ 11:1-43	☐ 12:1-33	☐ 13:1-34	☐ 14:1-31
43	☐ 15:1-34	☐ 16:1—17:24	☐ 18:1-46	☐ 19:1-21	☐ 20:1-43	☐ 21:1—22:53	☐ 2 Kings 1:1-18
44	☐ 2:1—3:27	☐ 4:1-44	☐ 5:1—6:33	☐ 7:1-20	☐ 8:1-29	☐ 9:1-37	☐ 10:1-36
45	☐ 11:1—12:21	☐ 13:1—14:29	☐ 15:1-38	☐ 16:1-20	☐ 17:1-41	☐ 18:1-37	☐ 19:1-37
46	☐ 20:1—21:26	☐ 22:1-20	☐ 23:1-37	☐ 24:1—25:30	☐ 1 Chron 1:1-54	☐ 2:1—3:24	☐ 4:1—5:26
47	☐ 6:1-81	☐ 7:1-40	☐ 8:1-40	☐ 9:1-44	☐ 10:1—11:47	☐ 12:1-40	☐ 13:1—14:17
48	☐ 15:1—16:43	☐ 17:1-27	☐ 18:1—19:19	☐ 20:1—21:30	☐ 22:1—23:32	☐ 24:1—25:31	☐ 26:1-32
49	☐ 27:1-34	☐ 28:1—29:30	☐ 2 Chron 1:1-17	☐ 2:1—3:17	☐ 4:1—5:14	☐ 6:1-42	☐ 7:1—8:18
50	☐ 9:1—10:19	☐ 11:1—12:16	☐ 13:1—15:19	☐ 16:1—17:19	☐ 18:1—19:11	☐ 20:1-37	☐ 21:1—22:12
51	☐ 23:1—24:27	☐ 25:1—26:23	☐ 27:1—28:27	☐ 29:1-36	☐ 30:1—31:21	☐ 32:1-33	☐ 33:1—34:33
52	☐ 35:1—36:23	☐ Ezra 1:1-11	☐ 2:1-70	☐ 3:1—4:24	☐ 5:1—6:22	☐ 7:1-28	☐ 8:1-36

Reading Schedule for the Recovery Version of the Old Testament with Footnotes

Wk.	Lord's Day	Monday	Tuesday	Wednesday	Thursday	Friday	Saturday
53	9:1—10:44 ☐	Neh 1:1-11 ☐	2:1—3:32 ☐	4:1—5:19 ☐	6:1-19 ☐	7:1-73 ☐	8:1-18 ☐
54	9:1-20 ☐	9:21-38 ☐	10:1—11:36 ☐	12:1-47 ☐	13:1-31 ☐	Esth 1:1-22 ☐	2:1—3:15 ☐
55	4:1—5:14 ☐	6:1—7:10 ☐	8:1-17 ☐	9:1—10:3 ☐	Job 1:1-22 ☐	2:1—3:26 ☐	4:1—5:27 ☐
56	6:1—7:21 ☐	8:1—9:35 ☐	10:1—11:20 ☐	12:1—13:28 ☐	14:1—15:35 ☐	16:1—17:16 ☐	18:1—19:29 ☐
57	20:1—21:34 ☐	22:1—23:17 ☐	24:1—25:6 ☐	26:1—27:23 ☐	28:1—29:25 ☐	30:1—31:40 ☐	32:1—33:33 ☐
58	34:1—35:16 ☐	36:1-33 ☐	37:1-24 ☐	38:1-41 ☐	39:1-30 ☐	40:1-24 ☐	41:1-34 ☐
59	42:1-17 ☐	Psa 1:1-6 ☐	2:1—3:8 ☐	4:1—6:10 ☐	7:1—8:9 ☐	9:1—10:18 ☐	11:1—15:5 ☐
60	16:1—17:15 ☐	18:1-50 ☐	19:1—21:13 ☐	22:1-31 ☐	23:1—24:10 ☐	25:1—27:14 ☐	28:1—30:12 ☐
61	31:1—32:11 ☐	33:1—34:22 ☐	35:1—36:12 ☐	37:1-40 ☐	38:1—39:13 ☐	40:1—41:13 ☐	42:1—43:5 ☐
62	44:1-26 ☐	45:1-17 ☐	46:1—48:14 ☐	49:1—50:23 ☐	51:1—52:9 ☐	53:1—55:23 ☐	56:1—58:11 ☐
63	59:1—61:8 ☐	62:1—64:10 ☐	65:1—67:7 ☐	68:1-35 ☐	69:1—70:5 ☐	71:1—72:20 ☐	73:1—74:23 ☐
64	75:1—77:20 ☐	78:1-72 ☐	79:1—81:16 ☐	82:1—84:12 ☐	85:1—87:7 ☐	88:1—89:52 ☐	90:1—91:16 ☐
65	92:1—94:23 ☐	95:1—97:12 ☐	98:1—101:8 ☐	102:1—103:22 ☐	104:1—105:45 ☐	106:1-48 ☐	107:1-43 ☐
66	108:1—109:31 ☐	110:1—112:10 ☐	113:1—115:18 ☐	116:1—118:29 ☐	119:1-32 ☐	119:33-72 ☐	119:73-120 ☐
67	119:121-176 ☐	120:1—124:8 ☐	125:1—128:6 ☐	129:1—132:18 ☐	133:1—135:21 ☐	136:1—138:8 ☐	139:1—140:13 ☐
68	141:1—144:15 ☐	145:1—147:20 ☐	148:1—150:6 ☐	Prov 1:1-33 ☐	2:1—3:35 ☐	4:1—5:23 ☐	6:1-35 ☐
69	7:1—8:36 ☐	9:1—10:32 ☐	11:1—12:28 ☐	13:1—14:35 ☐	15:1-33 ☐	16:1-33 ☐	17:1-28 ☐
70	18:1-24 ☐	19:1—20:30 ☐	21:1—22:29 ☐	23:1-35 ☐	24:1—25:28 ☐	26:1—27:27 ☐	28:1—29:27 ☐
71	30:1-33 ☐	31:1-31 ☐	Eccl 1:1-18 ☐	2:1—3:22 ☐	4:1—5:20 ☐	6:1—7:29 ☐	8:1—9:18 ☐
72	10:1—11:10 ☐	12:1-14 ☐	S.S 1:1-8 ☐	1:9-17 ☐	2:1-17 ☐	3:1-11 ☐	4:1-8 ☐
73	4:9-16 ☐	5:1-16 ☐	6:1-13 ☐	7:1-13 ☐	8:1-14 ☐	Isa 1:1-11 ☐	1:12-31 ☐
74	2:1-22 ☐	3:1-26 ☐	4:1-6 ☐	5:1-30 ☐	6:1-13 ☐	7:1-25 ☐	8:1-22 ☐
75	9:1-21 ☐	10:1-34 ☐	11:1—12:6 ☐	13:1-22 ☐	14:1-14 ☐	14:15-32 ☐	15:1—16:14 ☐
76	17:1—18:7 ☐	19:1-25 ☐	20:1—21:17 ☐	22:1-25 ☐	23:1-18 ☐	24:1-23 ☐	25:1-12 ☐
77	26:1—:21 ☐	27:1-13 ☐	28:1-29 ☐	29:1-24 ☐	30:1-33 ☐	31:1—32:20 ☐	33:1-24 ☐
78	34:1-17 ☐	35:1-10 ☐	36:1-22 ☐	37:1-38 ☐	38:1—39:8 ☐	40:1-31 ☐	41:1-29 ☐

Reading Schedule for the Recovery Version of the Old Testament with Footnotes

Wk.	Lord's Day	Monday	Tuesday	Wednesday	Thursday	Friday	Saturday
79	42:1-25	43:1-28	44:1-28	45:1-25	46:1-13	47:1-15	48:1-22
80	49:1-13	49:14-26	50:1—51:23	52:1-15	53:1-12	54:1-17	55:1-13
81	56:1-12	57:1-21	58:1-14	59:1-21	60:1-22	61:1-11	62:1-12
82	63:1-19	64:1-12	65:1-25	66:1-24	Jer 1:1-19	2:1-19	2:20-37
83	3:1-25	4:1-31	5:1-31	6:1-30	7:1-34	8:1-22	9:1-26
84	10:1-25	11:1—12:17	13:1-27	14:1-22	15:1-21	16:1—17:27	18:1-23
85	19:1—20:18	21:1—22:30	23:1-40	24:1—25:38	26:1—27:22	28:1—29:32	30:1-24
86	31:1-23	31:24-40	32:1-44	33:1-26	34:1-22	35:1-19	36:1-32
87	37:1-21	38:1-28	39:1—40:16	41:1—42:22	43:1—44:30	45:1—46:28	47:1—48:16
88	48:17-47	49:1-22	49:23-39	50:1-27	50:28-46	51:1-27	51:28-64
89	52:1-34	Lam 1:1-22	2:1-22	3:1-39	3:40-66	4:1-22	5:1-22
90	Ezek 1:1-14	1:15-28	2:1—3:27	4:1—5:17	6:1—7:27	8:1—9:11	10:1—11:25
91	12:1—13:23	14:1—15:8	16:1-63	17:1—18:32	19:1-14	20:1-49	21:1-32
92	22:1-31	23:1-49	24:1-27	25:1—26:21	27:1-36	28:1-26	29:1—30:26
93	31:1—32:32	33:1-33	34:1-31	35:1—36:21	36:22-38	37:1-28	38:1—39:29
94	40:1-27	40:28-49	41:1-26	42:1—43:27	44:1-31	45:1-25	46:1-24
95	47:1-23	48:1-35	Dan 1:1-21	2:1-30	2:31-49	3:1-30	4:1-37
96	5:1-31	6:1-28	7:1-12	7:13-28	8:1-27	9:1-27	10:1-21
97	11:1-22	11:23-45	12:1-13	Hosea 1:1-11	2:1-23	3:1—4:19	5:1-15
98	6:1-11	7:1-16	8:1-14	9:1-17	10:1-15	11:1-12	12:1-14
99	13:1—14:9	Joel 1:1-20	2:1-16	2:17-32	3:1-21	Amos 1:1-15	2:1-16
100	3:1-15	4:1—5:27	6:1—7:17	8:1—9:15	Obad 1:1-21	Jonah 1:1-17	2:1—4:11
101	Micah 1:1-16	2:1—3:12	4:1—5:15	6:1—7:20	Nahum 1:1-15	2:1—3:19	Hab 1:1-17
102	2:1-20	3:1-19	Zeph 1:1-18	2:1-15	3:1-20	Hag 1:1-15	2:1-23
103	Zech 1:1-21	2:1-13	3:1-10	4:1-14	5:1—6:15	7:1—8:23	9:1-17
104	10:1—11:17	12:1—13:9	14:1-21	Mal 1:1-14	2:1-17	3:1-18	4:1-6

Reading Schedule for the Recovery Version of the New Testament with Footnotes

Wk.	Lord's Day	Monday	Tuesday	Wednesday	Thursday	Friday	Saturday
1	Matt 1:1-2	1:3-7	1:8-17	1:18-25	2:1-23	3:1-6	3:7-17
2	4:1-11	4:12-25	5:1-4	5:5-12	5:13-20	5:21-26	5:27-48
3	6:1-8	6:9-18	6:19-34	7:1-12	7:13-29	8:1-13	8:14-22
4	8:23-34	9:1-13	9:14-17	9:18-34	9:35—10:5	10:6-25	10:26-42
5	11:1-15	11:16-30	12:1-14	12:15-32	12:33-42	12:43—13:2	13:3-12
6	13:13-30	13:31-43	13:44-58	14:1-13	14:14-21	14:22-36	15:1-20
7	15:21-31	15:32-39	16:1-12	16:13-20	16:21-28	17:1-13	17:14-27
8	18:1-14	18:15-22	18:23-35	19:1-15	19:16-30	20:1-16	20:17-34
9	21:1-11	21:12-22	21:23-32	21:33-46	22:1-22	22:23-33	22:34-46
10	23:1-12	23:13-39	24:1-14	24:15-31	24:32-51	25:1-13	25:14-30
11	25:31-46	26:1-16	26:17-35	26:36-46	26:47-64	26:65-75	27:1-26
12	27:27-44	27:45-56	27:57—28:15	28:16-20	Mark 1:1	1:2-6	1:7-13
13	1:14-28	1:29-45	2:1-12	2:13-28	3:1-19	3:20-35	4:1-25
14	4:26-41	5:1-20	5:21-43	6:1-29	6:30-56	7:1-23	7:24-37
15	8:1-26	8:27—9:1	9:2-29	9:30-50	10:1-16	10:17-34	10:35-52
16	11:1-16	11:17-33	12:1-27	12:28-44	13:1-13	13:14-37	14:1-26
17	14:27-52	14:53-72	15:1-15	15:16-47	16:1-8	16:9-20	Luke 1:1-4
18	1:5-25	1:26-46	1:47-56	1:57-80	2:1-8	2:9-20	2:21-39
19	2:40-52	3:1-20	3:21-38	4:1-13	4:14-30	4:31-44	5:1-26
20	5:27—6:16	6:17-38	6:39-49	7:1-17	7:18-23	7:24-35	7:36-50
21	8:1-15	8:16-25	8:26-39	8:40-56	9:1-17	9:18-26	9:27-36
22	9:37-50	9:51-62	10:1-11	10:12-24	10:25-37	10:38-42	11:1-13
23	11:14-26	11:27-36	11:37-54	12:1-12	12:13-21	12:22-34	12:35-48
24	12:49-59	13:1-9	13:10-17	13:18-30	13:31—14:6	14:7-14	14:15-24
25	14:25-35	15:1-10	15:11-21	15:22-32	16:1-13	16:14-22	16:23-31
26	17:1-19	17:20-37	18:1-14	18:15-30	18:31-43	19:1-10	19:11-27

Handwritten note (top margin): Mon. Arn + Jade

Reading Schedule for the Recovery Version of the New Testament with Footnotes

Wk.	Lord's Day	Monday	Tuesday	Wednesday	Thursday	Friday	Saturday
27	Luke 19:28-48 ☐	20:1-19 ☐	20:20-38 ☐	20:39—21:4 ☐	21:5-27 ☐	21:28-38 ☐	22:1-20 ☐
28	22:21-38 ☐	22:39-54 ☐	22:55-71 ☐	23:1-43 ☐	23:44-56 ☐	24:1-12 ☐	24:13-35 ☐
29	24:36-53 ☐	John 1:1-13 ☐	1:14-18 ☐	1:19-34 ☐	1:35-51 ☐	2:1-11 ☐	2:12-22 ☐
30	2:23—3:13 ☐	3:14-21 ☐	3:22-36 ☐	4:1-14 ☐	4:15-26 ☐	4:27-42 ☐	4:43-54 ☐
31	5:1-16 ☐	5:17-30 ☐	5:31-47 ☐	6:1-15 ☐	6:16-31 ☐	6:32-51 ☐	6:52-71 ☐
32	7:1-9 ☐	7:10-24 ☐	7:25-36 ☐	7:37-52 ☐	7:53—8:11 ☐	8:12-27 ☐	8:28-44 ☐
33	8:45-59 ☐	9:1-13 ☐	9:14-34 ☐	9:35—10:9 ☐	10:10-30 ☐	10:31—11:4 ☐	11:5-22 ☐
34	11:23-40 ☐	11:41-57 ☐	12:1-11 ☐	12:12-24 ☐	12:25-36 ☐	12:37-50 ☐	13:1-11 ☐
35	13:12-30 ☐	13:31-38 ☐	14:1-6 ☐	14:7-20 ☐	14:21-31 ☐	15:1-11 ☐	15:12-27 ☐
36	16:1-15 ☐	16:16-33 ☐	17:1-5 ☐	17:6-13 ☐	17:14-24 ☐	17:25—18:11 ☐	18:12-27 ☐
37	18:28-40 ☐	19:1-16 ☐	19:17-30 ☐	19:31-42 ☐	20:1-13 ☐	20:14-18 ☐	20:19-22 ☐
38	20:23-31 ☐	21:1-14 ☐	21:15-22 ☐	21:23-25 ☐	Acts 1:1-8 ☐	1:9-14 ☐	1:15-26 ☐
39	2:1-13 ☐	2:14-21 ☐	2:22-36 ☐	2:37-41 ☐	2:42-47 ☐	3:1-18 ☐	3:19—4:22 ☐
40	4:23-37 ☐	5:1-16 ☐	5:17-32 ☐	5:33-42 ☐	6:1—7:1 ☐	7:2-29 ☐	7:30-60 ☐
41	8:1-13 ☐	8:14-25 ☐	8:26-40 ☐	9:1-19 ☐	9:20-43 ☐	10:1-16 ☐	10:17-33 ☐
42	10:34-48 ☐	11:1-18 ☐	11:19-30 ☐	12:1-25 ☐	13:1-12 ☐	13:13-43 ☐	13:44—14:5 ☐
43	14:6-28 ☐	15:1-12 ☐	15:13-34 ☐	15:35—16:5 ☐	16:6-18 ☐	16:19-40 ☐	17:1-18 ☐
44	17:19-34 ☐	18:1-17 ☐	18:18-28 ☐	19:1-20 ☐	19:21-41 ☐	20:1-12 ☐	20:13-38 ☐
45	21:1-14 ☐	21:15-26 ☐	21:27-40 ☐	22:1-21 ☐	22:22-29 ☐	22:30—23:11 ☐	23:12-15 ☐
46	23:16-30 ☐	23:31—24:21 ☐	24:22—25:5 ☐	25:6-27 ☐	26:1-13 ☐	26:14-32 ☐	27:1-26 ☐
47	27:27—28:10 ☐	28:11-22 ☐	28:23-31 ☐	Rom 1:1-2 ☐	1:3-7 ☐	1:8-17 ☐	1:18-25 ☐
48	1:26—2:10 ☐	2:11-29 ☐	3:1-20 ☐	3:21-31 ☐	4:1-12 ☐	4:13-25 ☐	5:1-11 ☐
49	5:12-17 ☐	5:18—6:5 ☐	6:6-11 ☐	6:12-23 ☐	7:1-12 ☐	7:13-25 ☐	8:1-2 ☐
50	8:3-6 ☐	8:7-13 ☐	8:14-25 ☐	8:26-39 ☐	9:1-18 ☐	9:19—10:3 ☐	10:4-15 ☐
51	10:16—11:10 ☐	11:11-22 ☐	11:23-36 ☐	12:1-3 ☐	12:4-21 ☐	13:1-14 ☐	14:1-12 ☐
52	14:13-23 ☐	15:1-13 ☐	15:14-33 ☐	16:1-5 ☐	16:6-24 ☐	16:25-27 ☐	1 Cor 1:1-4 ☐

Reading Schedule for the Recovery Version of the New Testament with Footnotes

Wk.	Lord's Day	Monday	Tuesday	Wednesday	Thursday	Friday	Saturday
53	1 Cor 1:5-9	1:10-17	1:18-31	2:1-5	2:6-10	2:11-16	3:1-9
54	3:10-13	3:14-23	4:1-9	4:10-21	5:1-13	6:1-11	6:12-20
55	7:1-16	7:17-24	7:25-40	8:1-13	9:1-15	9:16-27	10:1-4
56	10:5-13	10:14-33	11:1-6	11:7-16	11:17-26	11:27-34	12:1-11
57	12:12-22	12:23-31	13:1-13	14:1-12	14:13-25	14:26-33	14:34-40
58	15:1-19	15:20-28	15:29-34	15:35-49	15:50-58	16:1-9	16:10-24
59	2 Cor 1:1-4	1:5-14	1:15-22	1:23—2:11	2:12-17	3:1-6	3:7-11
60	3:12-18	4:1-6	4:7-12	4:13-18	5:1-8	5:9-15	5:16-21
61	6:1-13	6:14—7:4	7:5-16	8:1-15	8:16-24	9:1-15	10:1-6
62	10:7-18	11:1-15	11:16-33	12:1-10	12:11-21	13:1-10	13:11-14
63	Gal 1:1-5	1:6-14	1:15-24	2:1-13	2:14-21	3:1-4	3:5-14
64	3:15-22	3:23-29	4:1-7	4:8-20	4:21-31	5:1-12	5:13-21
65	5:22-26	6:1-10	6:11-15	6:16-18	Eph 1:1-3	1:4-6	1:7-10
66	1:11-14	1:15-18	1:19-23	2:1-5	2:6-10	2:11-14	2:15-18
67	2:19-22	3:1-7	3:8-13	3:14-18	3:19-21	4:1-4	4:5-10
68	4:11-16	4:17-24	4:25-32	5:1-10	5:11-21	5:22-26	5:27-33
69	6:1-9	6:10-14	6:15-18	6:19-24	Phil 1:1-7	1:8-18	1:19-26
70	1:27—2:4	2:5-11	2:12-16	2:17-30	3:1-6	3:7-11	3:12-16
71	3:17-21	4:1-9	4:10-23	Col 1:1-8	1:9-13	1:14-23	1:24-29
72	2:1-7	2:8-15	2:16-23	3:1-4	3:5-15	3:16-25	4:1-18
73	1 Thes 1:1-3	1:4-10	2:1-12	2:13—3:5	3:6-13	4:1-10	4:11—5:11
74	5:12-28	2 Thes 1:1-12	2:1-17	3:1-18	1 Tim 1:1-2	1:3-4	1:5-14
75	1:15-20	2:1-7	2:8-15	3:1-13	3:14—4:5	4:6-16	5:1-25
76	6:1-10	6:11-21	2 Tim 1:1-10	1:11-18	2:1-15	2:16-26	3:1-13
77	3:14—4:8	4:9-22	Titus 1:1-4	1:5-16	2:1-15	3:1-8	3:9-15
78	Philem 1:1-11	1:12-25	Heb 1:1-2	1:3-5	1:6-14	2:1-9	2:10-18

Reading Schedule for the Recovery Version of the New Testament with Footnotes

Wk.	Lord's Day	Monday	Tuesday	Wednesday	Thursday	Friday	Saturday
79	☐ Heb 3:1-6	☐ 3:7-19	☐ 4:1-9	☐ 4:10-13	☐ 4:14-16	☐ 5:1-10	☐ 5:11—6:3
80	☐ 6:4-8	☐ 6:9-20	☐ 7:1-10	☐ 7:11-28	☐ 8:1-6	☐ 8:7-13	☐ 9:1-4
81	☐ 9:5-14	☐ 9:15-28	☐ 10:1-18	☐ 10:19-28	☐ 10:29-39	☐ 11:1-6	☐ 11:7-19
82	☐ 11:20-31	☐ 11:32-40	☐ 12:1-2	☐ 12:3-13	☐ 12:14-17	☐ 12:18-26	☐ 12:27-29
83	☐ 13:1-7	☐ 13:8-12	☐ 13:13-15	☐ 13:16-25	☐ James 1:1-8	☐ 1:9-18	☐ 1:19-27
84	☐ 2:1-13	☐ 2:14-26	☐ 3:1-18	☐ 4:1-10	☐ 4:11-17	☐ 5:1-12	☐ 5:13-20
85	☐ 1 Pet 1:1-2	☐ 1:3-4	☐ 1:5	☐ 1:6-9	☐ 1:10-12	☐ 1:13-17	☐ 1:18-25
86	☐ 2:1-3	☐ 2:4-8	☐ 2:9-17	☐ 2:18-25	☐ 3:1-13	☐ 3:14-22	☐ 4:1-6
87	☐ 4:7-16	☐ 4:17-19	☐ 5:1-4	☐ 5:5-9	☐ 5:10-14	☐ 2 Pet 1:1-2	☐ 1:3-4
88	☐ 1:5-8	☐ 1:9-11	☐ 1:12-18	☐ 1:19-21	☐ 2:1-3	☐ 2:4-11	☐ 2:12-22
89	☐ 3:1-6	☐ 3:7-9	☐ 3:10-12	☐ 3:13-15	☐ 3:16	☐ 3:17-18	☐ 1 John 1:1-2
90	☐ 1:3-4	☐ 1:5	☐ 1:6	☐ 1:7	☐ 1:8-10	☐ 2:1-2	☐ 2:3-11
91	☐ 2:12-14	☐ 2:15-19	☐ 2:20-23	☐ 2:24-27	☐ 2:28-29	☐ 3:1-5	☐ 3:6-10
92	☐ 3:11-18	☐ 3:19-24	☐ 4:1-6	☐ 4:7-11	☐ 4:12-15	☐ 4:16—5:3	☐ 5:4-13
93	☐ 5:14-17	☐ 5:18-21	☐ 2 John 1:1-3	☐ 1:4-9	☐ 1:10-13	☐ 3 John 1:1-6	☐ 1:7-14
94	☐ Jude 1:1-4	☐ 1:5-10	☐ 1:11-19	☐ 1:20-25	☐ Rev 1:1-3	☐ 1:4-6	☐ 1:7-11
95	☐ 1:12-13	☐ 1:14-16	☐ 1:17-20	☐ 2:1-6	☐ 2:7	☐ 2:8-9	☐ 2:10-11
96	☐ 2:12-14	☐ 2:15-17	☐ 2:18-23	☐ 2:24-29	☐ 3:1-3	☐ 3:4-6	☐ 3:7-9
97	☐ 3:10-13	☐ 3:14-18	☐ 3:19-22	☐ 4:1-5	☐ 4:6-7	☐ 4:8-11	☐ 5:1-6
98	☐ 5:7-14	☐ 6:1-8	☐ 6:9-17	☐ 7:1-8	☐ 7:9-17	☐ 8:1-6	☐ 8:7-12
99	☐ 8:13—9:11	☐ 9:12-21	☐ 10:1-4	☐ 10:5-11	☐ 11:1-4	☐ 11:5-14	☐ 11:15-19
100	☐ 12:1-4	☐ 12:5-9	☐ 12:10-18	☐ 13:1-10	☐ 13:11-18	☐ 14:1-5	☐ 14:6-12
101	☐ 14:13-20	☐ 15:1-8	☐ 16:1-12	☐ 16:13-21	☐ 17:1-6	☐ 17:7-18	☐ 18:1-8
102	☐ 18:9—19:4	☐ 19:5-10	☐ 19:11-16	☐ 19:17-21	☐ 20:1-6	☐ 20:7-10	☐ 20:11-15
103	☐ 21:1	☐ 21:2	☐ 21:3-8	☐ 21:9-13	☐ 21:14-18	☐ 21:19-21	☐ 21:22-27
104	☐ 22:1	☐ 22:2	☐ 22:3-11	☐ 22:12-15	☐ 22:16-17	☐ 22:18-21	☐

Week 1 — Day 4   Today's verses

Matt. ...Moses, because of your hardness of
19:8 heart, allowed you,...but from the beginning it has not been so.

Eph. But holding to truth in love, we may grow
4:15-16 up into Him in all things, who is the Head,
Christ, out from whom all the Body...
causes the growth of the Body unto the
building up of itself in love.

Date

Week 1 — Day 5   Today's verses

Lev. ...Moses took some of its blood and put *it*
8:23 on the lobe of Aaron's right ear and on the
thumb of his right hand and on the big toe
of his right foot.

Date

Week 1 — Day 6   Today's verses

Lev. No meal offering that you present to Jeho-
2:11 vah shall be made with leaven, for you
shall not burn any leaven or any honey as
an offering by fire to Jehovah.

Date

Week 1 — Day 1   Today's verses

1 Tim. Even as I exhorted you...to remain in
1:3-4 Ephesus in order that you might charge
certain ones not to teach different things
nor to give heed to myths and unending
genealogies, which produce questionings
rather than God's economy, which is in
faith.

Date

Week 1 — Day 2   Today's verses

John God is Spirit, and those who worship Him
4:24 must worship in spirit and truthfulness.
2 Tim. The Lord be with your spirit. Grace be
4:22 with you.

Date

Week 1 — Day 3   Today's verses

Eph. ...The church, which is His Body, the full-
1:22-23 ness of the One who fills all in all.

Date

Week 2 — Day 4   Today's verses

1 Tim. This is good and acceptable in the sight of
2:3-4 our Savior God, who desires all men to be
saved and to come to the full knowledge
of the truth.

Prov. Buy truth, and do not sell it; / Buy wisdom
23:23 and instruction and understanding.

Psa. The opening of Your words gives light, /
119:130 Imparting understanding to the simple.

Date

Week 2 — Day 5   Today's verses

Psa. Behold, You delight in truth in the inward
51:6 parts; / And in the hidden part You would
make known wisdom to me.

Col. Let the word of Christ dwell in you richly
3:16 in all wisdom, teaching and admonishing
one another with psalms and hymns and
spiritual songs, singing with grace in your
hearts to God.

Date

Week 2 — Day 6   Today's verses

1 Tim. But if I delay, I write that you may know
3:15-16 how one ought to conduct himself in
the house of God, which is the church of
the living God, the pillar and base of the
truth. And confessedly, great is the mystery of godliness: He who was manifested
in the flesh, / Justified in the Spirit, / Seen
by angels, / Preached among the nations, /
Believed on in the world, / Taken up in
glory.

2 Pet. And many will follow their licentious-
2:2 ness, because of whom the way of the
truth will be reviled.

Date

Week 2 — Day 1   Today's verses

John And you shall know the truth, and the
8:32 truth shall set you free.

2 Tim. Be diligent to present yourself approved
2:15 to God, an unashamed workman, cutting
straight the word of the truth.

3 John For I rejoiced greatly at the brothers' com-
3 ing and testifying to your steadfastness in
the truth, even as you walk in truth.

Date

Week 2 — Day 2   Today's verses

2 Pet. Therefore I will be ready always to remind
1:12 you concerning these things, even though
you know them and have been established in the present truth.

3 John I have no greater joy than these things,
4 that I hear that my children are walking in
the truth.

8 We therefore ought to support such ones
that we may become fellow workers in
the truth.

Rev. And I saw the holy city, New Jerusalem,
21:2 coming down out of heaven from God,
prepared as a bride adorned for her husband.

Date

Week 2 — Day 3   Today's verses

John Jesus said to him, I am the way and the
14:6 reality and the life; no one comes to
the Father except through Me.

18:37 ...For this I have been born, and for this
I have come into the world, that I would
testify to the truth. Everyone who is of the
truth hears My voice.

2 Tim. In meekness correcting those who
2:25 oppose, if perhaps God may give them
repentance unto the full knowledge of the
truth.

Date

Week 3 — Day 4

	Today's verses
1 Cor. 1:10	Now I beseech you, brothers, through the name of our Lord Jesus Christ, that you all speak the same thing and *that* there be no divisions among you, but *that* you be attuned in the same mind and in the same opinion.
Col. 1:18	And He is the Head of the Body, the church; He is the beginning, the Firstborn from the dead, that He Himself might have the first place in all things.
John 17:14, 17	I have given them Your word.... Sanctify them in the truth; Your word is truth.

Date _____

Week 3 — Day 5

	Today's verses
John 17:23	I in them, and You in Me, that they may be perfected into one, that the world may know that You have sent Me and have loved them even as You have loved Me.
1 Cor. 12:18	But now God has placed the members, each one of them, in the body, even as He willed.
2 Cor. 10:13	...We will not boast beyond *our* measure but according to the measure of the rule which the God of measure has apportioned to us, to reach even as far as you.

Date _____

Week 3 — Day 6

	Today's verses
Eph. 4:12	For the perfecting of the saints unto the work of the ministry, unto the building up of the Body of Christ.
1 Cor. 16:10	...If Timothy comes, see that he is with you without fear; for he is working the work of the Lord, even as I am.
12:24	...But God has blended the body together...

Date _____

Week 3 — Day 1

	Today's verses
Eph. 4:3-4	Being diligent to keep the oneness of the Spirit in the uniting bond of peace: one Body and one Spirit, even as also you were called in one hope of your calling.
1 Cor. 12:12-13	For even as the body is one and has many members, yet all the members of the body, being many, are one body, so also is the Christ. For also in one Spirit we were all baptized into one Body...

Date _____

Week 3 — Day 2

	Today's verses
John 17:21-22	That they all may be one; even as You, Father, are in Me and I in You, that they also may be in Us; that the world may believe that You have sent Me. And the glory which You have given Me I have given to them, that they may be one, even as We are one.

Date _____

Week 3 — Day 3

	Today's verses
John 8:12	...Jesus spoke to them, saying, I am the light of the world; he who follows Me shall by no means walk in darkness, but shall have the light of life.
Rev. 21:23	And the city has no need of the sun or of the moon that they should shine in it, for the glory of God illumined it, and its lamp is the Lamb.
22:1	And he showed me a river of water of life....
John 17:11	...Holy Father, keep them in Your name, which You have given to Me, that they may be one even as We are.
1 Cor. 16:19	The churches of Asia greet you....

Date _____

Week 4 — Day 6   Today's verses

Acts 5:20 ...Go and stand in the temple and speak to the people all the words of this life.

2 Cor. 4:5 For we do not preach ourselves but Christ Jesus as Lord, and ourselves as your slaves for Jesus' sake.

Week 4 — Day 5   Today's verses

Jer. 15:19 ...If you bring out the precious from the worthless, / You will be as My mouth....

Psa. 25:14 The intimate counsel of Jehovah is to those who fear Him....

Acts 6:4 But we will continue steadfastly in prayer and in the ministry of the word.

Week 4 — Day 4   Today's verses

Prov. 4:18 But the path of the righteous is like the light of dawn, / Which shines brighter and brighter until the full day.

Rev. 21:7 He who overcomes will inherit these things, and I will be God to him, and he will be a son to Me.

1 John 1:6-7 If we say that we have fellowship with Him and yet walk in the darkness, we lie and are not practicing the truth; but if we walk in the light as He is in the light, we have fellowship with one another, and the blood of Jesus His Son cleanses us from every sin.

Week 4 — Day 3   Today's verses

1 Cor. 14:23-24 If...the whole church comes together,... and all speak in tongues, and some unlearned *in tongues* or unbelievers enter, will they not say that you are insane? But if all prophesy and some unbeliever or unlearned person enters, he is convicted by all, he is examined by all.

26 ...Whenever you come together, each one has a psalm, has a teaching, has a revelation, has a tongue, has an interpretation. Let all things be done for building up.

Week 4 — Day 2   Today's verses

1 Cor. 14:1 Pursue love, and desire earnestly spiritual *gifts*, but especially that you may prophesy;

3-4 ...He who prophesies speaks building up and encouragement and consolation to men....He who prophesies builds up the church.

Week 4 — Day 1   Today's verses

Num. 11:29 ...Oh that all Jehovah's people were prophets, that Jehovah would put His Spirit upon them!

1 Cor. 14:31 For you can all prophesy one by one that all may learn and all may be encouraged.

Week 5 — Day 4

Today's verses

John 6:56 He who eats My flesh and drinks My blood abides in Me and I in him.

John 15:7 If you abide in Me and My words abide in you, ask whatever you will, and it shall be done for you.

Exo. 30:36-37 And you shall beat some of it very fine, and put some of it before the Testimony in the Tent of Meeting, where I will meet with you; it shall be to you most holy. And the incense which you shall make, you shall not make for yourselves according to its composition; it shall be holy to you for Jehovah.

Date

Week 5 — Day 5

Today's verses

Exo. 30:7, 9 And Aaron shall burn on it fragrant incense.... You shall not offer any strange incense on it....

Lev. 10:1 And Nadab and Abihu, the sons of Aaron, each took his censer, and put fire in them and laid incense on it, and they presented strange fire before Jehovah, which He had not commanded them.

1 Tim. 2:8 I desire therefore that men pray in every place, lifting up holy hands, without wrath and reasoning.

Date

Week 5 — Day 6

Today's verses

John 15:5 I am the vine; you are the branches.... Apart from Me you can do nothing.

1 Cor. 2:14-15 But a soulish man does not receive the things of the Spirit of God, for they are foolishness to him and he is not able to know *them* because they are discerned spiritually. But the spiritual man discerns all things, but he himself is discerned by no one.

Date

Week 5 — Day 1

Today's verses

Heb. 8:1-2 ...We have such a High Priest, who sat down on the right hand of the throne of the Majesty in the heavens, a Minister of the holy places, even of the true tabernacle, which the Lord pitched, not man.

Col. 3:1 If therefore you were raised together with Christ, seek the things which are above, where Christ is, sitting at the right hand of God.

1:9 Therefore we also, since the day we heard of *it*, do not cease praying and asking on your behalf that you may be filled with the full knowledge of His will in all spiritual wisdom and understanding.

Date

Week 5 — Day 2

Today's verses

Exo. 30:1 And you shall make an altar on which to burn incense...

Heb. 7:25 Hence also He is able to save to the uttermost those who come forward to God through Him, since He lives always to intercede for them.

Rev. 8:3-4 And another Angel came and stood at the altar, having a golden censer, and much incense was given to Him to offer with the prayers of all the saints upon the golden altar which was before the throne. And the smoke of the incense went up with the prayers of the saints out of the hand of the Angel before God.

Date

Week 5 — Day 3

Today's verses

Rom. 8:26-27 Moreover, in like manner the Spirit also joins in to help *us* in our weakness, for we do not know for what we should pray as is fitting, but the Spirit Himself intercedes for *us* with groanings which cannot be uttered. But He who searches the hearts knows what the mind of the Spirit is, because He intercedes for the saints according to God.

Eph. 6:18-19 ...Praying at every time in spirit and watching unto this in all perseverance and petition concerning all the saints, and for me, that utterance may be given to me in the opening of my mouth, to make known in boldness the mystery of the gospel.

Date

Week 6 — Day 4   Today's verses

1 Cor. Now I beseech you, brothers, through the
1:10 name of our Lord Jesus Christ, that you all speak the same thing and *that* there be no divisions among you, but *that* you be attuned in the same mind and in the same opinion.

11:19 For there must even be parties among you, that those who are approved may become manifest among you.

Week 6 — Day 5   Today's verses

Acts Therefore, King Agrippa, I was not dis-
26:19 obedient to the heavenly vision.

Eph. And to enlighten all *that they may see*
3:9 what the economy of the mystery is, which throughout the ages has been hidden in God, who created all things.

Prov. Where there is no vision, the people cast
29:18 off restraint....

Week 6 — Day 6   Today's verses

1 Pet. Shepherd the flock of God among you,
5:2-4 overseeing not under compulsion but willingly, according to God; not by seeking gain through base means but eagerly...and when the Chief Shepherd is manifested, you will receive the unfading crown of glory.

2:25 For you were like sheep being led astray, but you have now returned to the Shepherd and Overseer of your souls.

Week 6 — Day 1   Today's verses

2 Cor. Who has also made us sufficient as minis-
3:6 ters of a new covenant, *ministers* not of the letter but of the Spirit; for the letter kills, but the Spirit gives life.

4:1 Therefore having this ministry as we have been shown mercy, we do not lose heart.

Week 6 — Day 2   Today's verses

1 Tim. Even as I exhorted you, when I was going
1:3-4 into Macedonia, to remain in Ephesus in order that you might charge certain ones not to teach different things,...which produce questionings rather than God's economy, which is in faith.

Week 6 — Day 3   Today's verses

2 Cor. But we will not boast beyond *our* mea-
10:13 sure but according to the measure of the rule which the God of measure has apportioned to us, to reach even as far as you.

1 Pet. If you have tasted that the Lord is good.
2:3